The ENGLISH VILLAGE

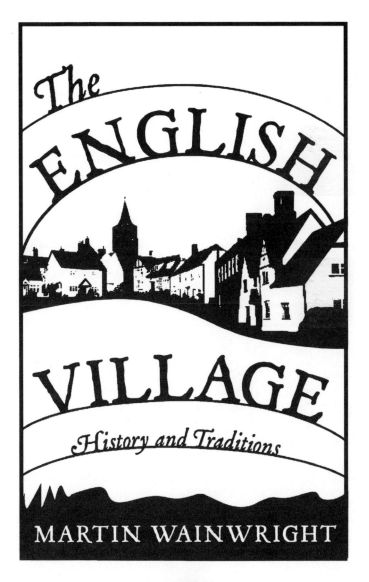

The ENGLISH VILLAGE

History and Traditions

MARTIN WAINWRIGHT

Michael O'Mara Books Ltd

First published in Great Britain in 2011 by
Michael O'Mara Books Limited
9 Lion Yard
Tremadoc Road
London SW4 7NQ

A CIP catalogue record for this book is available
from the British Library.

Papers used by Michael O'Mara Books Limited are natural,
recyclable products made from wood grown in sustainable forests.
The manufacturing processes conform to the environmental
regulations of the country of origin.

ISBN: 978-1-84317-712-8 in hardback print format
ISBN: 978-1-84317-794-4 in EPub format
ISBN: 978-1-84317-795-1 in Mobipocket format

3 5 7 9 10 8 6 4 2

Designed and typeset by www.glensaville.com

Printed and bound in Great Britain by Clays Ltd, St Ives plc

www.mombooks.com

CONTENTS

INTRODUCTION

'Few things are more pleasant than a village graced with a good church and a good pub,' wrote John Hillaby, one of my predecessors as a journalist on *The Guardian*. He was an enthusiastic walker who tramped round England discovering such delights, entranced as much by the manor houses, cottages and greens which add to the loveliness of so many countryside corners, as by the curiosities: ancient festivities, contorted carvings to scare off witches, or the stocks and gallows which remind us of the darker side of rural life.

Hillaby was a townie by birth – like me, a son of Leeds – but he and I both spent happy boyhood hours discovering how the virtues of the village are embedded in the urban round, and have been since our forebears moved from the country to the town – in my case from centuries of agricultural labouring in the North Yorkshire village of Well. I grew up in Adel, a comfy suburb of Leeds which Hillaby knew well, and in his *Journey through Britain*, he describes how its modest landmarks – the 'Slavering Babby' fountain, the Norman church and the 'Treasure Field' where relics were unearthed from a Roman army camp – told of a very ancient past.

Adel's name alone was a temptation for a city boy to find out more about the English village; it comes from the Anglo-Saxon for 'a filthy place', which was satisfactory for a rebellious teenager in the Sixties. The conformity of 1950s Britain was easing and the po-faced attitudes of well-to-do suburbs were under siege. When my grandparents moved into Adel in the 1930s, they were puzzled by the local vicar who called to take tea and asked them where they intended to be between October and March. 'Here,' replied my grandfather. 'But no one stays in Adel during the winter,' replied the vicar.

Times have changed. Adel remains prosperous but has grown much larger and few of its residents now think of spending all winter in Eastbourne or the Riviera, like so many amply paunched Yorkshire swallows. And so the story which began with the Romans tramping between London and York and needing somewhere to bivouac continues to evolve, as it does in another 'filthy place' just down the road – the Bradford suburb of Idle, home of the celebrated Idle Working Men's Club, whose name has the same origins as Adel but has come to be pronounced and spelt differently.

Collecting these facts like a magpie is thoroughly enjoyable, as is pitching into the vigorous debates which surround village life – past, present and future I have got stuck in myself and am ready for those who disagree, if not sanguine about the chances of coming to any absolutely certain conclusion. After all, I was born on the edge of Horsforth in Leeds, and I went to school in Colwall in Herefordshire, both of which firmly believe themselves to be the largest village in England. There are plenty of other claimants to the title and I am sure that none of them will ever back down.

I would like to thank my wife Penny, whose native St John's Wood in North London was once the hamlet its name suggests, for her patience as I clicked away on the computer and interrupted her with exclamations such as: 'Goodness, did you know there used to be a village called Dailymail?' (Read on . . .) I have been greatly encouraged and helped by Mathew Clayton and Toby Buchan of Michael O'Mara Books, and I am also grateful to James Empringham and Glen Saville for their jacket and text designs, respectively, to Aubrey Smith for his atmospheric illustrations, and to Rowena Anketell, Laura Buchan, Sue Gard and Andrew John for their work on the text and the index. But any mistakes are all my own.

CHAPTER ONE

FIFTEEN CENTURIES YOUNG

Townfolk know pleasures, country people joys.
MINNA ANTRIM (1861–1950)

Britain rushes around on its bypasses and motorways. Rapid roads and trains connect city to city, home to office, school-collection to shops. The traffic lights have gone green, the circle and slant of the derestricted sign allows the speedometer to flick to 70. Was that a field, some cows, a wood, a farm? Whatever, it's gone.

But then the cars and lorries jam, or autumn leaves block the line, and quietly and gently an older pattern of England steals back into its ancient and astonishingly little-altered place. What do those beguiling signs mean, inviting you to somewhere, something, maybe even someone called Huttons Ambo, The Alconburys or Mavis Enderby? Why go to the bog-standard motorway services when the satnav flashes up an icon for the Cottage of Content near Ross-on-Wye or the George at Stamford whose tag reads: 'Three kings have stayed here, as well as one of the fattest Englishmen ever – Daniel Lambert, who weighed 52 stone.' And didn't someone famous find that his train stopped unexpectedly at Adlestrop (alas, the station was closed in 1966)? Wasn't their curiosity just like yours?

Get off, branch off, turn off, and the greenery of village

England enfolds you with the certainty and confidence of settlements which have survived for up to a millennium and a half, and in some cases more. Devastation has often visited them in the form of the Black Death, civil war, evictions and the collapse of harvests. But a spell seems to girdle their familiar template of church and manor house, green and mill stream, tavern, beacon, war memorial, pond and stocks. Even where a town or city has rolled outwards and engulfed the ancient buildings themselves, road signs keep the past alive: Southfield Square, Chapel Close, Sheep Lane.

They touch something equally certain in millions of visitors. We may not have been here before, but our grandparents or their grandparents or *their* grandparents almost certainly led a life circumscribed by the seasons, rotation of crops and the demands of living in a close-knit community. Perhaps this was in The Alconburys, a cluster of hamlets just off the A1M north of Huntingdon, or at Mavis Enderby in Lincolnshire, whose shared sign with a neighbouring village is often converted by wags to read: 'To Old Bolingbroke and Mavis Enderby – the gift of a son.' Or it may have been somewhere very different in geographical terms: a life in thatched rondavel huts along the coast of West Africa or in a mountain hamlet in the Punjab. But the essence is there in every case, because the village way of life was so simple and the way that almost all of humanity lived for so long.

It has a special resonance in England, even among the ghosts of the relatively few communities which failed. Between today's thriving villages which have adjusted successfully to enormous economic and social change, you will occasionally find hummocky graveyards marking the sites of their lost counterparts; places where the plague, enclosures or even the whim of a powerful landlord who wanted an uncluttered view led to the abandonment of farms and homes. But here too, the essence of a village is so ingrained that the traditional features and patterns can still be seen. Only the larks and Marbled White butterflies now live at Wharram Percy in the Yorkshire Wolds, but a visitor can walk above the buried streets and work out where each of the familiar buildings stood. Drought conditions in the Lake District see the skeletal remains of Mardale Green emerge from the falling waters of Haweswater. Here was the church, there the pub, and behind them the grazing for the ponies which raced every summer at the Mardale fair.

The English countryside has also been fought over, brutalized and exploited from humanity's first arrival, and our means of changing things are today so devastating that the threat of irreversible damage to landscape, flora and fauna is a constant. But the scars of tragedy at battlefields such as Towton near Tadcaster, where in 1461 more Englishmen – 30,000 – died than at any other single place in the country, have long been engulfed by what the seventeenth-century poet Andrew Marvell called 'a green thought in a green shade'. The red-and-white 'York and Lancaster' rose runs riot over the hedges leading down to the Cock beck. No one is out of walking distance of such greenery and who does not relish that? For all that the English cluster more closely in towns and conurbations than any other European nation apart from the space-starved Dutch, we have a dreamy love of the countryside implanted in our national character. And the idyll within that dream is the village.

'Blood runs thicker than water and nothing is as thick as English village blood,' says Sir Simon Jenkins, chairman of the National Trust, contemplating the way in which we imagine these small communities to represent life at its best. 'An English village is like a medieval monastery, a place apart yet blessed with an innate goodness that trickles down to all society.' Is this a myth, or a partial truth? That is a question which has been asked for at least 1,600 years.

When did it all start? Were there villages in prehistoric Britain? We cannot be sure but little evidence has yet been found of settled communities. Rather, there were transitory camps for nomadic herdsfolk, flimsy dwellings which a tribe or group of families were ready to leave in the face of plague or invasion, dangers which threatened them all year round. Alfred Wainwright's Coast-to-Coast walking route threads through a slope of gentle dips and small mounds covered with rough grass which were once a typical example: the settlement at Severals above the valley of Smardale Gill and the Scandal Beck. Excitable archaeologists describe this lonely perch on the limestone plateau as the Manchester of the Bronze Age.

Then came the Romans, bringing civil order, roads and baths. But villages? No. Even in the imperial heartland of Italy the countryside was organized around large villas, the equivalent of the biggest of Europe's later stately homes. Family, labourers and slaves lived together in a unitary complex, a sprawling mansion with courts and outbuildings all in the ownership of the *dominus*, or master of the clan. In conquered Britain, this pattern soon emerged. If there were native hutments on the fringe of each mansion-farm, they were even more transitory than those which had gone before.

So it is the Anglo-Saxons, arriving in the fourth century AD, to whom we owe the pattern of settlements that we see today, and it is back to their time that the lineage of church, manor, mill and cottages can be directly traced. Rudyard Kipling put this into verse after immersing himself in the shadowy era of the legions' departure in AD 410 and the pirates of the 'Saxon shore' before the Vikings swept in, for books such as *Puck of Pook's Hill*. He wrote:

Behind the feet of the legions and before the Northmen's ire
Rudely but greatly begat they the body of state and shire.

Each group of invaders from northern Germany stuck with the habits of their home country, choosing a site for their Ing, Thwaite or By – all terms for a village – with an eye to the long term. The majority were built close to means of communication, along ridges, in valleys, or at the edge of a navigable river but high enough to avoid winter floods. This was important to the extraordinary longevity of England's villages. Today's roads follow the routes of military roads built from the capital originally designed to quell potentially rebellious regions or to counter invasions from Scotland and Wales. The sheer number of bypasses in the country and the importance of the word in our modern vocabulary are similar evidence of how closely the village and the highway have always been intertwined.

But Anglo-Saxon villages were not defensive places. They ignored the prehistoric tradition of the hill fort and the *castra*, or military camp, of the Romans. They were accessible, even vulnerable. From the Viking invasions onwards, many were sacked and burned and temporarily abandoned, but the villagers almost always returned and began again. They would have understood the feelings of Lord Dunsany, a celebrated novelist in the 1940s, who wrote an anthem for the Home Guard which began:

> *Give us for badge what some child's hand*
> *Might gather in our fields.*
> *Give us no star of blazonry*
> *Of Crown or crest, but let it be*
> *Rather some simple blend*
> *Of Traveller's Joy and bryony,*
> *Or such wild blooms as feed the bee*
> *On hills that we defend.*

The village has never been a physical fortress. It is the ideals which it represents which have been the inspiration for defence and the reason why the pattern of rural settlements established between AD 410 and 1066 survives to this day.

Fertile, level and well-watered ground was reserved for grazing domestic animals or growing crops, so the land chosen by the Anglo Saxons for their dwellings was often inferior.

Architecture was similarly practical. Most villagers lived in modest two-roomed huts or cabins, half for the family, the other half as a byre for their animals, with a 16-foot opening to admit a pair of yoked cattle. Modest, usually thatched churches often served a similar dual purpose on a communal basis, if large numbers of cattle or sheep needed shelter in rough weather. The same could even be true of the largest domestic building, the hall from which ruled the clan chief, or thane. The surrounding countryside was used generously; every simple home was endowed with plentiful land to ensure a viable living.

The Norman Conquest overturned the Saxon ruling elite but absorbed the social order. In the place of the thane came the baron or knight-at-arms. Instead of a hall, he ruled more often from a fortified stockade which in time could became a keep, a pele tower, a crenellated manor house or even a castle. Military duties and the expansionist, aggressive nature of the Norman state and Catholic Church frequently took the actual lord of the manor away from his home, leaving a bailiff to rule in his place. These middlemen were often out for themselves and a byword for thieving and injustice. The great story of Robin Hood fighting for villagers' rights against the usurpers of their true lords, is an amalgam of hundreds of smaller local stories of injustice.

The other central pillar of English village life was the church, whose organization had gone hand in hand with the Saxons' establishment of their kingdoms and shires. The concept of the parish fitted seamlessly with secular arrangements, down to the biblical foundations of the tithe system. Every villager surrendered a portion of their produce to the needs of the poor, via the church, for the good of their souls, just as they did to the thane and then the baron in return for guarantees of civil order and protection. Church and state together offered help when age, illness or mischance left a villager unable to cope.

Local priests were also at the baron or knight's right hand when it came to the structures of civil power. The Normans were more than comfortable with Saxon divisions of the shire into wapentakes, literally 'weapon takes', which were calculated on how many armed men an area could provide. To maintain the prowess of these arms, every village grew yew trees for longbows in the churchyard in order to protect young trees from rooting animals and animals from yew's poisonous berries. Each also had an area known as the Butts. Still remembered on many road signs or parish maps, this was set aside for compulsory archery practice after Matins on Sundays. As late as 1549 during one of many invasion scares, Bishop Latimer scolded Justices of the Peace who had been 'negligent in executing the law so that everyone has gone whoring into the towns instead of shooting in the fields'. He preached a whole sermon on the importance of archery as 'God's instrument whereby he hath given us many victories against our enemies'.

Throughout the medieval and Tudor period, virtuous priests such as Latimer were easy to find, but the legend of Robin Hood makes far more of the other sort: fat and greedy exploiters of the credulous who rashly allowed their wagons of coin and plate to take short cuts through Sherwood Forest. The emphasis given to such perversions of the social ideal is only partly an indicator of the way things were; it is more significant as a reinforcement of its opposite: the powerful, communal and ultimately national sense that village life was very precious and needed to be defended powerfully. The feudal system as refined by the Normans was rigid but within its boundaries it was also generous, especially by the standards of the time. There were usually a few sokemen, or freeholders from Saxon days, within large villages, even after the Conquest. And the ordinary serfs or villeins, while largely sticking to the simple Saxon design of two large rooms for their homes, were given plots called virgates, each of 30 acres, to cultivate in strips of different crops or use as pasture.

To call the medieval period between the Conquest and the Tudors a golden age is to be misty-eyed, but it is not difficult to see why the pattern became so deeply entrenched. Homes and farms were supported by a range of suppliers which grew as village products increased in number and sophistication: a mill, a joiner, a blacksmith, a forge. Each enjoyed the lord of the manor's protection in return for dues and each exacted their own dues from those who used their services.

It was over these four centuries, too, that the particular softness of the classic English village developed, as oak beams mellowed with age and wattle and daub settled into what the perceptive French writer Philippe Daudy described as a 'genial portliness' with low-slung cottages assuming a cosy, curled-up feline air beneath roofs like tilted hats. Joining the long procession of observers who see the village as one of the key motifs of the English character, he was entranced by the surrounding greenery, especially the village green with its pump, well and pond. 'We see only the lawns and gardens and forget the rain which makes them so green,' he wrote in his classic study *The English*. Within the Arcadian setting, a mutual bond of duties and obligations made for social harmony, reconciling two contradictory essentials of the English character: individualism and docility. The most humble and the most powerful lived very close together. The bonds were strong enough to survive the devastation of the Black Death in 1348, which killed an estimated third of England's then population of six million, and the Peasant's Revolt of 1381, which was less a cry for reform of feudalism than a howl against punitive taxes imposed by King Richard II on the still-devastated countryside.

But however agreeable to most English people, the village system was to suffer a series of man-made shocks, whose first rumble came when the monasteries buckled to the newly centralized Tudor state between 1536 and 1541. Ambitious locals on the make took advantage of the resulting uncertainty, the Crown's tacit encouragement of 'new gentry', and the sudden availability of a quarter of all registered land. Far grander manor houses than had been seen since Roman days suddenly became a new feature of the village, many built like Fountains Hall in North Yorkshire from the 'quarry' of high-quality stone available in abandoned abbeys. Land-grabbers also began a ruthless fencing-off of common land, creating enclosures to pasture animals, especially sheep, on a far greater scale than previously seen.

This was a triumph of individualism at odds with the feudal

contract, although some portents had been evident in the old system. Apparently rigid social contracts could be more flexible than the official account of manorial rolls and church tithe payments suggests. Many small-scale medieval farmers had found ways of renting and sometimes buying extra land. Families hired out their children as servants and used the income to pay for employees of their own. Modest entrepreneurs developed the cottage-weaving system, as well as quarrying, mining in one-man bell pits, and iron-forging, all of which established themselves as potential alternatives to farming. The term 'cottage industry' sounds picturesque compared to the Industrial Revolution's factory system with its enormous mills and automaton-like workforces. But it could be big business by anyone's standards, and a village full of looms going at full stretch was a noisy place. Not for nothing were the specialist textile cottagers in one of Cumbria's prettiest settlements known from the sixteenth century as 'the terrible knitters of Dent'.

This restlessness, and the flexing of muscles by the Tudors' 'new gentry' to which it led, had many influential opponents, including Sir Thomas More whose famous book *Utopia* laments of the enclosures: 'They stop the course of agriculture, destroying houses and towns, reserving only the churches, and enclose grounds that they may lodge their sheep in them.' There were frequent and bloody insurrections too, but behind the greed of the local grabbers was a calmer realization by government that ancient ways of farming no longer served an expanding nation. With outdated laws and customs being broken wholesale, the response was not to punish the lawbreakers but to change the law. By the eighteenth century, the ever-increasing enclosure of commons was led by Parliament.

And so the tenacious pattern of strip-farming finally came to an end, except in a handful of villages of which Laxton in Nottinghamshire is the finest surviving example. Here the farms stand beside the cottages as they always have, in a gentle straggle along the road to Egmanton and Toad Lane, with three vast open fields still divided into strips, administered by a Court Leet with its Clerk to the Gaits and Commons. Such institutions were everywhere in England before the enclosures, but by 1800 were virtually unknown.

The economic and social change was fundamental, although physically, the effects on the village landscape were less so. The most obvious was the relocation of large farms to outlying areas, so that listeners to Radio 4's indestructible rural soap opera *The Archers* correctly imagine David and Ruth at Home Farm to be based from large and well-equipped 'island' blocks of buildings separated from the centre of fictional Ambridge by their fields. In the village centres, there were fewer alterations – at least externally. But the loss of large individually tenanted holdings had dire consequences for living conditions within Philippe Daudy's 'genially portly, feline' homes.

Most villagers became landless tenants of an increasingly efficient and profitable system, living in properties let by the farmers for whom they worked. They were squeezed by a drive to make money, not just for comfort but to pay for the aggrandizement of manor houses, rectories and other homes of the rural well-to-do which began in the late seventeenth century.

The results were memorably portrayed by angry travellers such as William Cobbett, whose *Rural Rides* convinced him that slavery was alive and well in the shires as much as on the high seas between Europe, Africa and the West Indies. Visiting the fertile surroundings of Pewsey in Wiltshire in 1826, he wrote:

> *I have to express my deep shame, as an Englishman, at beholding the general extreme poverty of those who cause this vale to produce such quantities of food and raiment. This is, I verily believe it, the worst used labouring people upon the face of the earth. Dogs and hogs and horses are treated with more civility; and as to food and lodging, how gladly would the labourers change with them! This state of things never can continue many years! By some means or other there must be an end to it; and my firm belief is, that the end will be dreadful.*

Four years later, the Captain Swing riots saw vicious violence sweep through the supposedly soft and socially harmonious countryside of southern England. School history's long-standing tendency to focus on urban affairs, the Industrial Revolution and the notorious Peterloo Massacre, can obscure the fact that by the end of 1830, more than 2,000 men and women were in custody in the southern counties of England, awaiting trial for rural rioting. Nineteen were executed, 600 jailed for more than a year, and 500 transported to Australia as convicts for terms of between seven years and life. Peterloo had seen fifteen deaths and hundreds of injuries, but its legal consequences were only ten protesters tried, five acquitted and the longest sentence totalling just two years.

Cobbett and Captain Swing helped to bring political reform, but the remnants of Arcadia in village life could not be so simply restored by statute books. Their very gradual return began instead through the unlikely means of depopulation, as industry boomed and the obvious escape for any villager with energy and drive was to pack up and light out to the towns. The means to do so was helped by the creation first of the canal network, which transported hundreds of destitute families from East Anglia's countryside to the Lancashire and Yorkshire mills, and then by the railways. The effect of the latter was dramatic to an extent which conventional history has tended to overlook, as with the rural violence in the early nineteenth century, because in retrospect it proved a hiccough.

For some fifty years, villages which had relied on coach and wagon trade for both communication and an elaborate system of inns with high-arched carriage entrances – still a feature today – were all but deserted. Their economies were wrecked by the collapse of passing trade. In a series called *Rambles Around Manchester* in the 1880s, the *Manchester Guardian* described 'fields and meadows looking as unkempt and disused as if they had been ravaged by an invading army'. The author of the articles, Lieutenant-Colonel Sir George Tomkyns, later used his impressions to good effect in his book *The Battle of Dorking*, whose description of a fictional foreign invasion was so realistic that it helped to fuel the armaments race which culminated in the First World War.

The arrival of motor cars not only restored prosperity but took it to unprecedented levels, as the twentieth century brought blessings to villages on a scale which finally made those Arcadian impressions of hollyhocks, contented rustics and pink-cheeked lads and lasses a reality for most of the rural population.

Memorial to the battle of Towton (1461), North Yorkshire

The scars of the previous century remained, but gradually assumed the mantle of heritage, like Towton battlefield or, a new feature of almost every English village, the memorial to the dead of the two world wars. The progress of recovery was not uninterrupted; briefly in 1918 the flu pandemic seemed to threaten scenes reminiscent of the Black Death. Standing as a Conservative candidate in that year's general election, the future editor of the *Daily Telegraph*, Colin Coote, canvassed farmhouses in the Isle of Ely where he found the entire household dead. As he toured other villages in Cambridgeshire, he noted that not one was without its limbless or shell-shocked victims of the trenches. But the twentieth century's terrible twin convulsions were the final instrument in the creation of the English village as we know it today: they brought three great changes by transforming farming, establishing sound and healthy living conditions, and re-energizing parish democracy – the 'localism' of current political discussion – after the battering it had been given for at least three centuries.

The English village has never been as prosperous as it is today, but challenges do not fade away. Those of today include the withdrawal of many local services from the countryside, partly because of the continuing concentration of most of the population in towns or conurbations, but also in recognition of individual prosperity. People who lose out are those who are without their own transport or too old or too young to use it; and those without IT communications – a dwindling number and one which public computer services are working to ease. Novel arrangements have been introduced such as the 'telesurgeries' conducted over the Internet from Airedale general hospital in West Yorkshire to the village hall at Grassington, 25 miles away. The greater problems are those brought by success: the financial effects of ever more desirable housing and the pressure for new homes, so that ever more people can enjoy the English village ideal.

And it still is an ideal, and an immensely powerful one, as the recent history of a Cinderella group of villages in the former coalfields of county Durham eloquently illustrates. Famously, the privations of mining and its tradition of tough men combining against tough management have made 'pit villages' intensely communal. The battle of residents to save a score of decayed examples whose mines had closed, staggered the well-meaning planners of Durham County Council who had spent months designing a bright new future elsewhere.

The largely tenanted communities strung out towards the Pennines and the Northumberland border were classified in the mid-1950s as 'D-villages' which would be demolished and returned to agricultural land after their residents had been decanted to modern housing in Bishop Auckland or the new towns of Newton Aycliffe and Peterlee. The benign intentions of the solidly Labour council were highlighted by the second town's name, which honoured Peter Lee, a miner and Methodist preacher who was one of the industry's most respected union leaders in the late nineteenth and early twentieth century. But that didn't help.

The villagers were having none of it. As Peter Crookston describes in *The Pitmen's Requiem*, his moving history of the miners' brass-band 'hymn' 'Gresford' and its composer, Robert Saint, families in colliery-built housing at South Hetton, dilapidated nineteenth-century versions of the simple old village cottage which the council declared 'unfit for human habitation', led a revolt. Posters appeared in windows and on lamp posts saying 'Peterlee is a nightmare, not a dream.' There was a mass demonstration outside Bishop Auckland town hall and steady losses of Labour council seats led to anti-demolition Independents taking control of the district council in 1968.

Victory was finally sealed by other factors. The growth of commuting changed the area's economy and brought in new residents who worked with long-standing locals to repair houses and communal buildings and restore pride. The D-village policy was finally withdrawn in 1977 and public resources were redirected to helping with the renewal, creating the attractive mixture of homes and occupations which the villages boast today.

But the line had been held for a vital decade by twentieth-century versions of John Gray's 'village Hampden' who drew on 150 decades of tradition to refuse to change. It is no coincidence that the English speak of 'pit villages', almost always built around previous, long-settled parishes, while the transitory Americans, forever upping sticks and starting over, call their counterpart communities 'mining camps'. Durham had forgotten this, just as many of us, in our busy, scampering, urban lives, can forget too.

As the novelist and historian Sir Walter Besant wrote on first reading the great chronicler of village and countryside life, Richard Jefferies: 'Why, we must have been blind all our lives! Here were the most wonderful things possible going on under our very noses, but we saw them not.' From church to parish council meeting, it is good to be reminded just how much there is to relish.

CHAPTER TWO

THE BIG HOUSE

The cup of tea on arrival at a country house is a thing which, as a rule, I particularly enjoy. I like the crackling logs, the shaded lights, the scent of buttered toast, the general atmosphere of leisured cosiness.

P. G. (Sir Pelham Grenville) Wodehouse (1881–1975)

Since the time of the Norman castle or keep towering over its surrounding wattle-and-daub huts, the 'big house' has been a fundamental part of the quintessential English village scene, both in reality and in the nation's imagination. Its place in the community is so long-standing and so familiar, beside the church and cottages and surrounded by gardens and park, that fact and fiction have become hard to separate. Is Downton Abbey real, or Highclere Castle? Do the misty mansions of Turner's watercolours have a basis in fact, or are places such as Farnley Hall at Otley, where he painted so many of them, figments of the imagination?

The reality is there sure enough, with a fascinating history dating back to Roman times which illuminates the tenacious skill of the English at creating and maintaining country estates. The country's only original gift to world culture is often said to be landscape gardening and if that is true, it is appropriate. The gentry in the big house would shift Heaven, Earth and any amount of soil and vegetation to establish and keep their hold.

Equally enlightening is the cultural reaction of most English men and women to this state of affairs: an acceptance bordering on admiration for striking inequalities of wealth whose origins were often distinctly murky. Files of visitors touring the elegant Yorkshire mansion of Fountains Hall, whose unscrupulous builder stole the stones from the nearby abbey after the Reformation, murmur good-humouredly at such ruthlessness. They positively twinkle at the National Trust's Seaton Delaval Hall in Northumberland at the monument to John Delaval who died in 1775 'as a result of having been kicked in a vital organ by a chambermaid to whom he was paying his addresses'.

This feeling is so strong that many chroniclers of the village have become convinced that everyone accepts it, almost to the extent of singing the famous hymn 'All Things Bright and Beautiful' with the same innocent acceptance as children. The verse asserting that the Lord God made the rich man in his castle and the poor man at his gate, establishing both the high and lowly and 'ordering their estate' might go a little far, but in the 1930s Depression the writer Ralph Dutton mournfully surveyed decaying and even abandoned manor houses for which there was neither a family dowry nor a commercial market, and spoke of a feeling of 'sadness and incompleteness in a village in which the "big house" is derelict . . . a deep, spiritual sense of intangible loss which even the village socialist will probably share'.

If this sounds far-fetched, consider a case where socialists of a pretty determined character teamed up with the last of an ancient line of earls to try and protect an estate from opencast mining. The unlikely alliance in 1946 at Wentworth village near

Rotherham completely wrong-footed the Labour Government of Clement Attlee, recently elected with a huge majority, and its fiercely left-wing minister of fuel and power, Manny Shinwell. Dismissing the beautiful surroundings of Wentworth Woodhouse mansion as 'a nobleman's palace and pleasure grounds', he was astonished to learn of a press conference given by Joe Hall, Arthur Scargill's predecessor as president of the National Union of Mineworkers (NUM). Denouncing the plan to strip and mine almost up to the frontage of the vast house, one of the biggest and certainly the longest in England, Hall said:

It is sacrilege. Against all common sense. The miners of this area will go to almost any lengths rather than see Wentworth Woodhouse destroyed. It has taken at least a century to produce these lovely grounds and gardens. Yorkshire people cannot stand by and see it all devastated in a few weeks.

The miners actually threatened to strike; and the reasons were understandable to anyone who unpicked the long history of relations between the Earls of Fitzwilliam, whose personal wealth was far greater than anyone could conceivably need, and the villagers who often only just scraped by. The inequality was deplored by many, but the role of the family in this particular big house was acknowledged nevertheless. They were generous employers, their coal mines were a byword for safety and good management, and they welcomed everyone into the park (which Shinwell did in the end destroy, although restoration is now in prospect, more than half a century on.) During the furore, local supporters of the last Earl's campaign with the NUM recalled how they were allowed to skate on the frozen ornamental fountain ponds in winter, how £100 was offered to any batsman in the regular cricket matches on the main lawn who could break one of the hall's hundreds of windows (none ever did – the Fitzwilliams had checked that it was impossible), and how marquees had been erected on the same lawn during the 1926 General Strike to give free meals to miners and their families who had been obliged through union solidarity to walk out. None of this prevented satisfaction when the mansion finally passed into public use in the 1950s as a teacher training centre. But even then, the Fitzwilliams clung on in name. Rotherham council's new institution was called Lady Mabel College after a family member who was a devoted worker for the Labour Party in the early twentieth century.

The fact that such affection could exist at the very height of discrepancies between the big house and the surrounding little ones, which has seldom been greater than at Wentworth, helps an understanding of the origins of the social contract which led to centuries of acceptance and often friendship between the rich man in his castle and the poor man at his gate. It began with realpolitik under the Romans, whose relations with the conquered Britons were wholly pragmatic: don't cause trouble and we will protect you and keep order. The legions never fully settled, and their Saxon successors reverted to a softer and more communal relationship between nobles and freemen, where distinctions were very much less. But the Roman pattern then returned under the Normans and this time the conquest was permanent. The contract was also very much more specific, in terms of feudal duties by the villagers and obligations on the lord of the manor; and it was fortified and lent the spiritual power of potential heavenly reward or eternal damnation by the close involvement of the village priest and church. It also placed real burdens on the wealthy man. In the event of real danger, the entire village was guaranteed entry to his fortified home and provisions while they were there.

To begin with, the Norman intruders kept like the Romans to such strongholds and their military bases and castles, but after the defeat of the last rebellions in the north and by the phantom of the Isle of Ely, Hereward the Wake, arrangements gradually relaxed. The development of monasteries, which was one of the greatest enthusiasms of the French invaders, showed how useful it could be for everyone to have an efficient centre of farming and small businesses, from the woollen trade to forging iron, close to a village. The local baron or knight-at-arms was the obvious candidate to provide something smaller but similar.

Thus developed that most beguiling of English village concepts, the manor house with its demesne, a picture of cosy and well-organized rural life, with pastures, vegetable beds, fish ponds and the humble beginnings of landscape gardening shown in the ordering of land around the village to suit the needs of hunting and the chase. There was plenty of game available, and as the stories of Robin Hood repeatedly emphasize, very fierce laws against its poaching; but catching rabbits was not going to earn a stint in the stocks or worse, and the gradual development of hunting for hunting's sake forged another bond between the big house and the lesser ones.

Even today, opponents of hunting are often surprised by the genuine social mixture of country people who get involved. Whatever the rights and wrongs of animal welfare and cruelty arguments, the idea that hunters are just toffs is absurd. In the same way, the sensibly run manor house would always host communal village gatherings, from harvest homes with free food and drink provided, to galas, May Queen ceremonies and money-raising functions, opening the grounds and often the house. As those murmurs at Fountains Hall continue to show, people like nothing more than a peep behind the gentry's scenes, allied to the pleasure of visiting stately homes whose ancient owners are still around, with their clobber and family photos on display.

Philippe Daudy, the French journalist who observed the English so acutely while based in London, was lost in admiration for the way the National Trust made use of this relationship. He sought out the amendment to its constitution in 1937 which introduced the common and still continuing practice of allowing donor families to retain a flat. 'Here is one of those extraordinary English compromises which, collected in an anthology, might constitute the best possible handbook of political wisdom,' he wrote. 'Do visitors to National Trust properties resent the arrangement? On the contrary, most of them draw vicarious pleasure from the enchanted country house life which they imagine these leisured families to be leading, as they sip their tea on immaculately tended lawns.'

It is an indicator of the strength of the relationship, which was only very occasionally wrecked by rural riots or brutal behaviour by a landowner, that it survived the aggrandizement of the 'big house' which became commonplace from the eighteenth century, when England's long record of political convulsions at last eased and the rise to modern prosperity, through imperial expansion, the growth of industry and efficient capitalism, began. This saw a major change in many villages with the manor house, much larger than its neighbours but usually still on a similar scale, replaced by far grander buildings.

Owlpen Manor, Gloucestershire

There had been a modest precursor to this during the previous 150 years, when prosperous lords of the manor in areas such as East Anglia and the Cotswolds, where the woollen industry, larger-scale farming and fishing thrived, had embellished existing manors. Beautiful examples such as Owlpen Manor, of which the final additions were completed in 1616, followed the advice of a book called *Elements of Architecture* whose author, Sir Henry Wotton, was encouraged to publish because of the growing demand for finer country homes.

His advice in precis was to make sure that the manor house was not 'subject to any foggy noisomeness, from fens or marshes near adjoining, not indigested for want of Sun, not unexercised for want of view. Avoid malign influences as it may be earthquakes or contagions and do not let it be said, as it was of Mytelene: "a town in truth finely built but foolishly planted".' In its mellow setting on the wooded hillside of a steep Cotswold valley, Owlpen meets all these criteria and its plaudits in modern times include the Fodor guide's verdict: 'The loveliest place in England' and Prince Charles's judgement: 'The epitome of the English village.'

Sir Henry was inadequate, however, for the Georgian builders of the eighteenth century, whose reference books were Palladio and his disciples in England such as Lord Burlington of Chiswick House. Initially, their influence encouraged an approach well shown at Cothelstone in Somerset, where the landowner Edward Esdaile, who married the poet Shelley's daughter, decided that the lovely old manor house which had been in his family for three generations, was too old-fashioned and too close to neighbours. Typically for the time, he built a classically fronted mansion a mile or so outside the village, aloof in its park beneath gentle hills and sheltering woods. It was smart, but in the end the old manor proved the stouter survivor. It flourishes today as the country house hotel Cothelstone Manor, while the mansion,

Cothelstone House, was demolished in 1962.

Esdaile's move was not disruptive to his village, other than socially, but that was certainly not the case in the most ambitious of these grandiose projects. Competition to do better than the Joneses, or more accurately the Dukes of Jonesshire, infected the builders. News spread of such extraordinary tours de force as Stowe in Buckinghamshire, where the Temple family not only moved mountains but decorated the result with some fifty temples in accordance with their playfully punning scriptural motto *Templa quam dilecti* (How delightful are thy temples). Carried along by this fashion for transforming nature which was set and constantly encouraged by Lancelot 'Capability' Brown, Humphrey Repton and William Kent, the wealthiest new developers simply swept villages out of their new views. This happened at Newnham Courtney in Oxfordshire, Harewood in West Yorkshire, Kedleston in Derbyshire and more than fifty other places. Apart from plague and the collapse of local agriculture, it was the biggest single assault on the extraordinary ability of English villages to stay rooted to the spot where the Anglo-Saxons had first decided they should be.

Did it leave the astonished villagers homeless? Far from it. The sites of the transformations are instantly recognizable by the orderly development of neat new homes on the road nearest to the lord of the manor's new park. They were out of sight but certainly not out of mind. The new houses would have seemed brash and ill-adjusted to the timeless countryside around them – something which time has largely healed, although some examples including Harewood still smack of the barracks.

There was more than a touch of the regime still in force at Heslington estate village near York in the 1930s, where the rule was described to the writer Charles Kightly by a local pensioner some years later:

> *You had to behave yourself. You hadn't to cut ivy off your house because his Lordship liked to see it, and all t'houses were painted the same colour. The doors'd be red, or they had 'em all green another time, and windows had to be white. Estate used to buy paint and the tenants'd do painting.*

It was never freedom hall, but the relocated homes were immensely better-built, bigger, lighter and serviced with improved drainage, communal water supplies and the like. It is germane that one of the three great landscape gardeners who encouraged this process and also worked at Stowe, William Kent, had been a classic beneficiary of enlightened 'big house' behaviour himself.

As a boy in Bridlington on the Yorkshire coast in the 1690s, Kent showed unusual talent as an artist and was employed by the local squire to paint livery on new carriages – themselves part of the growing luxury of the 'big house'. He made himself useful more generally and his interest in both architecture and gardening encouraged the squire to pay for him to join a group of young gentry taking the traditional European tour. One of them was Thomas Coke, who was later made the first Earl of Leicester (fifth creation; other families have held the earldom), and he too recognized Kent's talent and used his wealth and influence to provide contacts. Others who benefited from this classic exercise of the rich man's obligations, which were felt especially strongly in villages' small and close communities, included the famous engraver Thomas Bewick and the father of chronometers and safe navigation at sea, John Harrison, whose first attempts at clock-making were encouraged by the Winn family at Nostell Priory, near Wakefield, now one of the National Trust's most popular houses.

Kent worked discreetly to encourage his patrons to look out for other talented young people in their local villages, but he could only go so far. Two obstacles to a universal adoption of enlightened fellowship between big house and village during these upheavals were commonplace, one unintentionally obstructive but the other the deliberate result of haughtiness and greed. The first was a result of the pampered upbringing of lords of the manor which made some of them ill at ease with their rougher neighbours. They were exceptions to the genial tradition of Squire Western in Henry Fielding's *Tom Jones* (1749) who much preferred the company in the taproom of the local pub to his fellow members of the county set. Famously ill-at-ease examples include the Duke of Somerset, who employed outriders to clear the local lanes of people when he went riding and, most extraordinarily, the 5th Duke of Portland at Welbeck Abbey in Nottinghamshire. Although a generous employer who was nicknamed 'the workman's friend', he was almost pathological about seclusion and constructed a famous series of tunnels through which he travelled his large estate, with smaller parallel ones for his staff.

The other category was different. An unpleasant example was Lord Ailesbury who in 1815 enclosed the last common land around the Wiltshire village of Burbage and in the process removed local rights to collect wood and house pigs in Savernake Forest which went back to before the Norman Conquest. Prolonged resistance led to the peer establishing the Tottenham Association, one of the first of a series of vigilante groups established by landowners to act as an unofficial police force against any villager trespassing on their newly fenced-off land. At their peak in the 1820s there were 400 in England, and the breadth of their remit can be seen by the list of actions declared punishable in 1821 by the Leekfrith Association for the Prosecution of Felons, a landowners' association established near Macclesfield in Cheshire:

> *Burglary, highway or footpad robbery. Wilful arson of a dwelling, barn, stable building, ricks, corn, grain, or hay. The maiming of horses, bulls, oxen, etc. sheep, pigs. Stealing corn, grain, hay, clover out of buildings, ricks, or stocks. Stealing cocks or turkeys, geese, ducks, hens, chickens, turnips, potatoes, carrots, cabbages or grass, wagons, implements of husbandry. Robbing any garden, milking any cow or purchasing or receiving stolen goods. Stealing doors, windows, gates, stiles, pens, freaks, rails, posts, hedges, hedge wood fuel of any sort, lime, iron, wood growing or fallen. Cutting, chopping down, breaking, destroying or carrying away timber trees, fruit trees, plants, underwood, gorse, furze, or heath. Damaging wagons, carts, plows, harrows. Taking any fish in any pond, brook or water belonging to us, the members of this association.*

Ailesbury's unpopularity increased when he decided in the same year as the Leekfrith declaration to spend £250,000 (£22 million at 2010 values) on enlarging his mansion. This provided some local employment but that was soon over and Ailesbury's peremptory ways and the striking contrast between his lavish home and his workers' cottages fuelled resentment. There were disturbances in all the villages where he had influence, which played their small part in the gradual movement towards political change which culminated in the Great Reform Bill of 1832.

Renishaw Hall, Derbyshire

In the long run, this movement was to transform the old relationships within the English village utterly, replacing paternalism – even in its most benign and unselfish forms – with the healthier modern attributes of equal status and mutual respect. The growth of taxation made life infinitely harder for old landed families which had lived on rents and left money matters to bailiffs and stewards. When Ralph Dutton (later the eighth Baron Sherborne, although the title died with him in 1985) wrote his 1935 elegy on the country house (which he thought would be more of an epitaph) the attrition of halls, manors and stately homes was widely reckoned terminal. In his introduction to the book, Osbert Sitwell, of the famous literary family at Renishaw in Derbyshire, lamented that even during the preparation of his text another two mansions close to his own had gone. One of them was Sutton Scarsdale, the gaunt ruin which overlooks the M1 motorway opposite Bolsover Castle and Hardwick Hall. Bought and gutted by a consortium of local businessmen, it was at least to have a ghostly half-life for many more years: its wooden panelling was sold to a Hollywood studio and used in many films set in fictitious English country homes.

But this decline was seldom accelerated by resentment, any more than the 'new squires' who today live in most of England's manors, halls and other large village houses, are considered unfairly wealthy or potential oppressors of their neighbours. In part, the unfailingly rich crop of colourful characters who lived in the big house helped. Who could take against Colonel James Harrison of Brandesburton Hall near Hornsea, who brought six pygmies back from an exploration in the Congo and then delighted villagers with a demonstration of their skill at shooting fleeing rabbits with bows and arrows? Or his near neighbours up the Yorkshire coast, the Stricklands of Boynton Hall, who kept up a family tradition of ornamenting everything with turkeys, including the local church pulpit whose lectern has the bird instead of an eagle? This habit stemmed from their ancestor William Strickland's fame as the man who brought the first turkey from America in 1542. His descendants inherited his doughtiness, continuing to live in the hall until the late 1950s and seeing it return to distant relatives in 1980.

This accounts in part for the easy-going pleasure which Phillipe Daudy noticed in visitors to houses run by the National Trust, whose ever-increasing estate is now third in size only to the Queen's and the lands of the Forestry Commission. And it is not sentimental to suggest that another ingredient has been the lasting effects of thousands of generous-hearted lords of the manor over the centuries. Their character was moulded in turn by the benign nature of the village community itself, of which they were the most fortunate members.

It is good to read accounts of a mutually respectful relationship, such as this one from a woman who lived in Burgh-on-Bain in Lincolnshire in the 1930s when Girsby Manor, the big house locally, was the home of Sir John and Lady Fox and laid on Christmas treats for the children. In her case, a collection of fifteen dolls was brought to her cottage every year by the Foxes' butler because she had asthma and could never attend the party. Describing this to the rural studies researcher Charles Kightly in the early 1980s, she remarked: 'Oh, they were very, very good were Girsby Manor. Burgh's been going down ever since they left. We thought a lot of Sir John and Lady Fox and they did of us. We were their people.'

CHAPTER THREE

GOD'S ACRE

A man he was to all the country dear,
And passing rich with forty pounds a year.
Remote from towns he ran his godly race,
Nor ever had changed, nor wished to change, his place.
OLIVER GOLDSMITH (1728–74)

The story of England is told in her village churches whose spires and towers are the first landmarks to catch the eye of any visitor to the countryside. In countless small details, from stained-glass panels to graffiti scratched on oak pews, the people's history is recorded in these modest but often superbly designed and ornamented local buildings. The job is done as thoroughly as the way that St Paul's Cathedral and Westminster Abbey, with all their pomp and circumstance, honour the deeds of the famous.

As well as catching the eye, the village church frequently gives the place its name: Church Fenton, Kirkoswald, Chapel Stile and the hundreds of places in Wales which start with Llan, the Welsh word for church. The church building itself is also part of a group which has been known as God's Acre since Saxon times. Appropriately enough it is a trinity: three in one and one in three is how this story is told.

The first part of it lies in the evidence of 1,600 years of architecture, from the huge half oak trunks which form the walls of Greensted church in Essex, not far from the end of the London Underground's Central line at Epping, to the startling modernism of 1930s churches in the pit villages of South Yorkshire's former coalfields. Inside them, the story continues on the memorials on the church walls and the curiosities of charity bequests, often lettered in gold on ostentatious wooden panels, which explain how local worthies left funds for the deserving poor, sometimes for their children's education, sometimes for a weekly loaf of bread.

The second part is to be found in God's Garden, the churchyard whose original role as a burial place has been superseded by its value as a nature reserve amid today's neatly tended flower beds and vegetable allotments beside regularly mown verges and busy roads. Among the wildflowers or sometimes the wilderness beyond the control of a congregation's faltering lawnmower rota, stand gravestones with marvellous names, moralistic epitaphs and occasional revealing evidence of past times such as mortmain – extra locks and bolts to protect a family vault from bodysnatchers employed by rogue medical schools. A whole book about village society is written here.

And the third part of the story is told in the vicarages, rectories and manses, and the character and memories of the parish priests and their Nonconformist colleagues who lived in them. They were usually educated men – and today, women – whose observations of village life are an invaluable part of history's long record. The most dutiful are probably under-represented because they were too busy caring for their flock, like the brave vicars at Eyam, Revd William Mompesson and Revd

Thomas Stanley, who took decisive action to isolate the hillside Derbyshire village in 1666 when cloth from London brought the plague. We know a lot about them and in consequence about the unifying forces and countervailing stresses of village life in their day, but not from their pens. They left history to others, and in their case it was written, because of the dramatic nature of the events. Countless other modest priests, and the work that they did, have no memorial, other than their influence on villagers and village life in their day.

The prominence and cost of English village churches dates from the earliest days, when the God-fearing culture of the Anglo-Saxons was reluctant to challenge the Lord's house by erecting more magnificent secular buildings. The thane would have his hall, and some of them were relatively imposing, but the best craftsmen were always directed to the church and the priest. Their work was modest compared to the glories of church architecture to come, but it was so sound and well executed that more than 400 churches with Saxon work survive, from St Mary the Virgin's at Little Abington in Cambridgeshire to St Peter's at Yaxham in Norfolk.

Alignment was the builders' first task and where possible, they chose to site the church so that it faced east, towards the dawn. This was not sacrosanct, unlike the exact calibration of the *mihrab* niche in mosques which faces Mecca, and topography or land availability also played their part. But the majority of village churches face east and have associated legends connected to the north, or 'Devil's side'. It is often the case that secular village events take place in the northern quarter of the graveyard, and some still have a 'devil's door' in their north wall, as at Worth in West Sussex and Kirkby Malham in North Yorkshire. This was traditionally left open during special services, particularly christenings, to encourage the evil one to scarper.

As the pride of the village, the church would also take the best building material, and the 10,000 standing today are a marvellous indicator of local geology: mellow red sandstone in Cumbria's Eden Valley, honey-coloured in the Cotswolds, and a blaze of almost luminous limestone or chalk in the Cheddar area of Somerset and inland from the Seven Sisters' cliffs and Beachy Head. Stonework naturally led successive builders' thoughts to carvings, and the wealth of their imagination, from Saxon days to the present, is overwhelming.

Church of St Mary and St David, Kilpeck, Herefordshire

A famous example is the twelfth-century church of St Mary and St David in Kilpeck, whose door and corbels are a riot of devils, sprites, the restless rural phantom known as the 'Green Man' and a hound beside a hare which both look astonishingly like their modern TV cartoon counterparts. Lewd and suggestive, officially to scare off devils but doubtless also to entertain the carvers and their audience, some of the work was defaced by a prudish Victorian lady of the manor. But she could not destroy the vigour and brio of the carving.

Stained glass was a legacy of the Romans and hundreds of fragments have been found at Monkwearmouth and Jarrow on Tyneside where the Saxon abbot Benedict Biscop brought French specialists in AD 675 to work on his new priory. These are the earliest examples of a craft which was to spread to almost every village church in the country, thanks to its beauty and convenience as a gift or memorial from wealthy patrons. Hence the thousands of windows dedicated to young medieval wives who died in childbirth, crusaders, and later the tragic victims of imperial expeditions and world wars. Many happier events are also recorded in the sunlit colours. One of the treats of visiting St Michael and All Angels' at Hubberholme in the Yorkshire Dales is hunting down the tiny panel in a large composite window, showing the railway bridge at the Victoria Falls in southern Africa. Its engineer, George Hobson, lived in this delectable spot, which J. B. Priestley called 'one of the smallest and pleasantest places in the world'.

Hubberholme church is one of many where visitors can also play 'hunt the mouse', a familiar game in hundreds of churches where wooden furnishings were made by Robert 'Mousey' Thompson, a craftsman who always hid a small, carved mouse in his work. There are countless variants on this, in terms of looking for birds, fish, angels and devils which church decorators added to everything from roof bosses to misericord seats – the narrow flip-up ledges which gave some comfort to choristers during long services during which they were not supposed to sit down.

Most of these adornments were the gift of wealthy village patrons, such as Sir William Trussell of Shottesbrooke in Berkshire who not only rebuilt the parish church after the Black Death but endowed a small college with a warden and five priests. In 1412 Dame Katerine of Burgh agreed to make 'the kirk of Ketericke [Catterick in North Yorkshire] all newe as werkmanship and mason craft will' and a century later at Lavenham in Suffolk, the Earl of Oxford unusually pooled his aristocratic resources with a classic example of 'new money', a local family called Spryng who had made a fortune from wool, to build the church of St Peter and St Paul.

Such embellishments are almost always recorded on plaques and inscriptions. An additional interest in exploring church interiors is to discover the extent of their opposite: iconoclasm, the religious ardour of Puritans which led them to destroy the 'vain, Popish show' of church decoration, as they held it to be, during the Protestant Reformation and again at the height of the English Civil War. Their motives were high-minded and can be understood to an extent if you attend a service in a large church where the rituals are conducted out of sight of the 'ordinary' congregation behind an ornate chancel screen. But the loss of beautiful work from their zealotry is incalculable and they spared little, once they had decided to act. At Winchester Cathedral, Oliver Cromwell's men loaded a cannon with supposed holy relics, and fired it through the stained-glass windows.

A curious example of village iconoclasm is at St Michael's church in Aldbourne, Wiltshire, where an ornate memorial to the Goddard family has eight kneeling figures, all with their daintily carved fingers chopped off. The damage was done during the Civil War, although there may have been an element of malice against a puffed-up family, who appear to have ordered high-blown figures which bear no resemblance to the people they commemorate and may well have been sold by another aristocratic household fallen on hard times. Aldbourne is in many other ways a typically fascinating English village church, from its Saxon site to its use in 1971 as a backdrop for the BBC TV hero Dr Who and his battle against aliens called the Daemons.

Another unhappy set of victims of Puritan zeal were the wall paintings which were common to hundreds of early English churches and performed the role of an enormous, brightly illustrated textbook to educate illiterate villagers. Unlike the clergy's tenacious hold on Latin scriptures, which led to the burning of Reformers who worked to get the Bible translated into English, these simple scenes from the Bible, often supplemented with local touches such as meadow flowers or Cotswold sheep and Hereford cattle, were used by priests to illustrate their sermons. Careful restoration has returned some

Church of St Agatha, Easby, North Yorkshire

to the light, with the removal of whitewash or render, and a few examples providentially survived without defacement.

There is a fine series at the little church of St Agatha at Easby in North Yorkshire, which crouches among yew trees and other greenery in the lea of Easby Abbey's ruins a mile out of Richmond. The paintings show Adam and Eve and other Old Testament characters in landscapes which have more than a touch of Yorkshire; the stories' morals of virtuous behaviour and obeying the Ten Commandments were all the more powerful for having some local context. This applies in a similar way to many memorials, which introduce deer, wildfowl and sometimes more ferocious but familiar beasts. On the stone walls of St Peter's church in Barnburgh, near Rotherham, is carved a wildcat. It recalls a fatal fight between one of the animals and the lord of the manor, Sir Percival Cresacre, in 1477, which ended with both dying in the church porch.

Such dangers are a thing of the past, but they remind us how closely the village church is linked to its graveyard, which first appeared in Saxon times as a burial ground but soon had sound financial reasons for wider use. Possession of a burial area entitled the local congregation to hold back a third of the tithe for repairs to the church fabric, money which would otherwise have gone to the priest or, more commonly, to church authorities higher up, including bishops such as Wilfrid of Ripon who were notorious for expensive tastes in food, wine, comfortable housing and rich vestments. Exercising this right was one of the early encouragements of the churchwarden system, which gave roots to a form of democracy in villages at a very early stage. Churchyards were important bastions against overmighty local chieftains in another way. They were known for many centuries as 'sanctuaries' because until the late medieval period, fugitives accused of anything except sacrilege and treason could claim immunity there.

Until the Reformation brought plainer customs, the village graveyard was often cultivated as a garden too. Today, the combination of old stones, freshly dug soil, abundant planting and ancient boundary walls is a paradise for wildlife, but in the medieval period, it sheltered flower gardens for posies – used as medicine and freshening smelly cottage rooms as much as for decoration – along with healing herbs and vegetables. There were many other practical uses for local people over the centuries. Borrowing gravestones for drying washing was widespread, benefiting from the combination of sunshine and warm stone, and children could play safely in the enclosed area. Ancient rotas in churches list the parishioners responsible for maintaining the boundary walls and fences. In her study *God's Acre*, Francesca Greenoak notes that there were all of eighty-one of them in Cowfold in Sussex in the sixteenth century, and fifty-six at Chiddingley, not far away.

The graveyard's abundant flora and fauna were also a stimulus to their minders, the clergy, whose role in amateur science has been a match for their care of souls. From the beginning, village priests were different from their flock, better educated and more enterprising; but often the narrow boundaries of a village community gave them too little to do. From the late medieval period onwards, many of them were learned graduates of Oxford and Cambridge who, as younger sons of county families, took church livings while their eldest brothers inherited the estate and the next in line went into the Forces. In the late eighteenth and early nineteenth century in particular, they found themselves in charge of parishes where churchgoing had dwindled to almost nothing because of clerical sloth and the rise of energetic Nonconformist churches such as the Methodists.

This proved posterity's gain, as the vicars immersed themselves in studying flora, insects, birds and village lore. They recorded more than a hundred different types of lichen on the ideal habitat of ancient tombstones. They encouraged the spread of species, such as the shining cranesbill which a nineteenth-century vicar brought with him to Holton-le-Moor in Lincolnshire when he moved from the plant's stronghold at Matlock on the edge of the Derbyshire Peak District. They have left a vast library of distinguished research and the prince of them all, Revd Gilbert White of Selborne in Hampshire, produced a masterpiece in his *Natural History of Selborne* which was published in 1789 and has never been out of print. Like many of his fellow clergy, he was an amateur, albeit a very knowledgeable one, but the vicars also included eminent professionals. In 1837 the professor of mineralogy and later botany at Cambridge University, Revd Prof John Henslow, decided to change course and take the living of an obscure Suffolk village called Hitcham. He was certainly not slothful, instituting many reforms, starting botany classes for the local children, and persuading the local farmers to use fertilizer. Unlike some other contemporary clergy, he also drew on his practical knowledge of natural history to become a mentor and great supporter of Charles Darwin. His contribution to science far outweighed his efforts on behalf of his minuscule flock.

The character of village priests has been a constant subject for debate across the centuries, matched by the incumbents' radically differing views of their job and flock. As early as 1301, the Bishop of Exeter felt obliged to conduct an audit of his parish priests, inviting their congregations to tell him privately of how well, or otherwise, they were being served. The evidence survives and is fascinating. The vicar of Clyst Honiton was considered 'an honest man but, alas, broken with age', while Randolph the chaplain at Dawlish had 'kept a concubine for ten years and though often rebuked, persisted with her incorrigibly'. In the same spirit, the Bishop of Norwich complained in 1362 of village rectors 'sub-contracting' their work to lay assistants who were 'rather day labourers than pastors'. William Langland, writing his *Vision of Piers Plowman* at the same time, contrasted the true Christian life with the character of a vicar called Sloth who was much better at hare-coursing than construing the Psalms. It was at this time, too, that the church felt obliged to pass a law which ruled that errors in Latin by ill-educated priests did not invalidate baptism.

As for the incumbents' views of their parishioners, these differed every bit as wildly over the years, and in doing so add illuminating evidence about the long history of village life. In the late eighteenth century, for example, the jovial curate of Lastingham on the edge of the wild North York Moors was so intimate with his parishioners that he got his young wife to take on the tenancy of the Blacksmith's Arms and played his violin and danced there on Sunday evenings. When this came to the attention of the authorities, the curate Revd Jeremiah Carter mounted a spirited defence: his stipend of only £20 a year needed supplementing for his family to survive, he told the archdeacon, and the pub tenancy was a convenient solution. As for the revelry, his flock often had to travel miles across the moors and his playing of the fiddle and leading a dance distracted them from 'heavy drinking and bad conversation'. The archdeacon was convinced and disciplinary action was withdrawn.

In complete contrast was the experience of Revd John Skinner, doing his dogged best in his parish of Camerton, near Bath, now a highly desirable village for commuters to the Georgian city or Bristol, but very different in the early and mid-nineteenth century.

His voluminous diaries record depressingly unprofitable dealings with intractably venal villagers, a catalogue of misery which caught the attention of Virginia Woolf. She wrote after reading Skinner's record: 'It would need a very rosy pen and a very kindly eye to make a smiling picture of life in this village.' And indeed, almost every page contains harrowing details of victims of Mr Purnell, the miserly magistrate, and Mrs and Mrs Hicks, the workhouse overseers who left a dying pauper without medical care so that 'maggots had bred in his flesh and eaten great holes in his body'. There is an account of the screams of a weak-minded widow of a drunk who had been locked in her cottage by Mr Purnell's officials and then fallen on the fire – Revd Skinner, passing by, heard her agonies and was unable to force an entry. Perhaps the entry with the most pathos in Skinner's forty years of chronicling village life, is the one in October 1809 when he writes:

> *While walking between churches into the village I met George Coombs, the local alehouse keeper, and fell into conversation. He does not attend worship and I asked him whether he had seen a building called a Church on his walk. Even this direct sally was unsuccessful as the landlord deflected the vicar's warning of damnation if he did not improve his ways by reply succinctly: 'Ah doesn't believe in Hell.'*

These stories show the nadir of village life at a time when it was dominated by unscrupulous large farmers and sapped by the Industrial Revolution's lure of enterprising families to the mill towns.

A constant tug on the consciences of the priests, who were always admonishing others for their shortcomings, was their own establishment in homes which were among the largest in the village. Rectories and vicarages which grew ever more spacious as the social standing of incumbents became more elevated and, especially after the high noon of Victoria's reign, they became expected to father as many children as the tribes of Israel. Changing times now see today's village clergyman ensconced as often as not in a modern bungalow while 'The Vicarage' or 'The Old Rectory' is one of the swankiest addresses after 'The Manor House' or 'The Old Hall'.

The principal difference between a vicar and a rector was that until clerical reforms in the late nineteenth century, the rector benefited personally from tithes and the vicar did not. Small wonder, then, that a Rectory Society was established in 2006 by the conservatively minded journalist Charles Moore, a former editor of the *Spectator* and *Daily* and *Sunday Telegraphs*. Its first members' outing was to a former rectory at Sarsden Glebe near Chipping Norton, designed by no less an expert than Humphrey Repton, replete with acres of parkland and rambling gardens. It was of a piece with similar properties such as Church House in Northiam, Sussex, which was sold in 2007 for £3.75 million, or the Old Rectory at Cossington in Leicestershire, a Grade II listed building dating from between the sixteenth and eighteenth centuries which Nikolaus Pevsner described as 'one of the best small domestic buildings in the county'. It was sold at the same time as Northiam's for £2.75 million, which also brought the buyer stables, a coach house flat and 35 acres of garden, including woodland and a lake.

Such establishments undoubtedly rivalled God's House in a way which would have appalled the Anglo-Saxons; and their lavish arrangements attracted satire from contemporaries. The witty traveller Celia Fiennes was astonished by the rectory garden at Banstead in Surrey whose incumbent had spent fifty years in his parish, devoting much more of his time to his garden than to his religious duties. She wrote in 1700:

> *His grass plots have stones of divers formes and sizes which he names Gods and Goddesses; and hedges and arbours of thorn so neatly cut. There are severall heads painted which were named Mogul Grand Seigneur, Cham of Tartary and Tsar of Muscovy. Another garden is Grass plots with yews and holly laurels and stones sett very thick, some very much bigger for officers. This is the whole Confederate army and their generals. Also he has a trumpeter, Hercules and Bacchus and a laurel hedge full seven feet wide.*

Alexander Pope was another visitor to village parsons who found their gardening hard to take, especially when it involved time-consuming trimming of those old churchyard familiars, yew trees. The poet wrote disparagingly of 'those who are so fond of evergreens', describing the trees as 'little ornaments driving out the nobler forest trees, pyramids of dark green continually repeated, not unlike a funeral procession'. He would have been exercised by the twentieth century's love affair with Leyland cypress.

This lavish self-indulgence fed the mixture of radicalism and austerity which established a different form of Christian worship as a permanent part of the English village scene. The Nonconformist chapel appealed to those who saw the established Church of England as an example of moral decay. The Anglicans were disliked for the rigid enforcement of the tithe, even when its clerical recipients had no need of the money which many of their parishioners could ill afford. The appeal of the Wesley brothers, and their counterparts among the Baptists and Unitarians, was increased by Church of England vicars such as Revd 'Spurting' Bullen of Eastwell in Yorkshire who hunted throughout his fifty-four-year incumbency and Revd Storey of Lockington in Leicestershire who staged a cockfight in his church with the Marquis of Hastings.

As a result, the Nonconformist chapel took its place in the English village landscape, usually a modest building which was all that its largely working-class or farm labourer congregation could afford, but with a simple beauty indoors. A delightful example is still in use for Sunday worship at the village of Wath-in-Nidderdale, a graceful five-sided building at the end of a terrace of cottages with a fine little organ and wooden gallery. This was luxury for denominations which initially had to contend with such strong disapproval from Government that their chapels were forbidden within six miles of an Anglican church. Until gentler measures prevailed, this led to remarkable places of worship such as the overhanging Buck Stone at Rawdon, near Leeds, where Baptists met on Sundays, rigging up a tent extension to the space beneath the rock face by cutting grooves in the stone for supporting poles, which can still be seen.

Dislike and suspicion of these breakaway churches was

initially intense among village Anglicans, with even the gentle Quakers cast into jail and ordained Church of England priests such as John Wesley regarded as renegades. The novels of George Eliot are instructive on the way that 'free church' ministers could be seen as outsiders and a threat. The nineteenth-century literary establishment was generally cautious about them; Jane Austen and the Brontë sisters were daughters of rural Anglican priests. And there was good reason to be worried. Methodism and the rise of organized labour marched hand-in-hand and the role of the Nonconformists' amateur 'local preachers' was important in preparing many untutored orators for future roles in the House of Commons.

More modestly, villages saw remarkable success from the eighteenth century onwards for utopian countryside sects with limited but very practical aims. A good example was the Dependents, a cooperative church founded in the late nineteenth century in Sussex by John Sirgood, a shoemaker and Methodist local preacher. Nicknamed the 'Cokelers' because of Sirgood's constant promotion of cocoa in place of alcohol, the group denied Anglican priests' spiritual authority and was an early focus of women's liberation. They have left a lasting memorial in the village of Northchapel – another place taking its name from its church – where the former Dependent cooperative store still stands. In its heyday before the First World War, it employed thirteen women in a village with a population of under 700, deliberately to save them from going into service. Others worked on Dependent-owned farms and in a thriving bakery.

Enthusiasm was ever a mark of such breakaway churches,

and the services in their chapels and gospel halls could involve an exaggerated version of the 'Praise the Lord!' exclamations of modern gospel churches. In the village of Woodhouse, near Halifax, for instance, a Methodist minister called Joseph Entwistle described with alarm how Sunday service 'went beyond all bounds of decency – such screaming and bawling, I never heard. Divided into small companies within the chapel, some singing, some praying, others praising, clapping of hands etc. All was confusion and Uproar, continuing until five o'clock in the morning.'

The racket was intolerable, said Entwistle; but there, perhaps, it made common cause with a final contribution of God's Acre to the English village. Of all the sounds most closely associated with the pastoral idyll, none are more evocative than church bells. Dating back to Saxon times, the traditional chimes and peals served for centuries not only as a summons to worship but a public clock; there were few other ways of marking the passage of time. One of the greatest controversies to involve the village churches of England took place during the Second World War when all bells were silenced so that they could be used, alongside the ancient beacon system, in the event of a Nazi invasion.

Reluctantly accepted at first, the silence imposed on the beautiful sound of pealing or chiming church bells became more and more controversial as the war ground on. The Archbishop of York led protests and managed to win two exceptions in 1942, once to mark the victory of El Alamein in North Africa and again at Christmas. By the following April, when rural MPs under pressure from their constituents raised the issue in Parliament, even the Prime Minister, Winston Churchill, sympathized, telling the Commons that in the unlikely event of the enemy storming ashore: 'I cannot help feeling that news of anything so serious would leak out.' The restrictions were eased, but it was not until Victory in Europe Day on 8 May 1945 that the right to ring bells at any time was restored, and the peal at Holy Trinity, Crockham Hill, the nearest church to Churchill's own country home at Chartwell, rang out once more.

CHAPTER FOUR

FESTIVALS AND FROLICS

Come lasses and lads, get leave of your dads,
And away to the Maypole hie,
For every he has got him a she,
And the fiddler's standing by.
ENGLISH TRADITIONAL (C. 1670)

The bonds within the English village between rich and poor, old and young, or long-standing families and newcomers have always been strengthened by communal occasions, an annual calendar of festivities linked to saints' days, the seasons or flimsy excuses to celebrate some local event or hero. The earliest ones were usually based on the church although often with roots going back to pre-Christian days, incorporating the mistletoe of the Druids at Christmas or timing All Souls and Hallowe'en with its spooky lanterns to coincide with the witches and demons' ceremony, Walpurgis Night.

Perhaps the most famous and long-lasting of these is the Beating of the Bounds of the parish by the congregation led by the priest, and young boys who would slash at the village's boundary markers and then be whipped themselves or bounced up and down on the border stones before getting consolation in the form of a halfpenny. These procedures were designed to din into the community's collective memory exactly where the boundary lay, to avoid encroachment by neighbouring landowners or disputes over the level of tithes or expenses for maintaining the church and graveyard.

The gallivanting could go on for as long as six days in larger villages and its wilder side reflected supposed origins in the Roman festival of Terminalia which honoured the god of boundaries whose name Terminus now has workaday associations with buses and trains. In medieval England, the rituals always ended with a feast known as a parish ale and things frequently degenerated. During Henry VIII's reign in the 1540s when anticlericalism was being whipped up by government agents in preparation for the seizure of the monasteries, a bishop condemned the way that 'these solemne and accustomable processions and supplications be nowe growen into a right foule and detestable abuse'.

The bishop was an exception. For most, the Beating of the Bounds was regarded with great affection and it continues in many parishes today. During its long history, there have always been prosperous villagers who looked back on their own experience as a whipping boy and left money to help the tradition continue. The strangest is at Leighton Buzzard where beer and plum rolls are distributed while the will of the man whose legacy provided them, a London merchant with local roots called Edward Wilkes, is read. During this ceremony one of the boys has to stand on his head under a stipulation in the bequest, again designed to make the ceremony, and the boundaries, unforgettable.

The ceremony had a religious purpose in addition to its

geographical importance at a time when there were no maps. Hymns and prayers relating to the annual cycle of crops were sung and appropriate passages from the Scriptures read at stopping points, a ritual which gave rise to familiar place names such as Gospel Oak. The intention was to invite God's blessing on the seedtime and in due course the harvest; and as a result the period in February when the Beating of the Bounds is carried out became known in the church calendar as rogation, from the Latin word meaning 'to ask'.

St Oswald's Church, Grasmere, Cumbria

A similar village tradition, Rush-bearing, played a part in the establishing of Harvest Festival as one of the most popular of church festivals, to the extent that the child outgrew its parent and is now much better-known. Only a smattering of modern villages continue the practice of renewing the rushes which were strewn on the earth floor of Anglo-Saxon and early Norman churches – a humdrum duty which, like many such, was made more appealing by the addition of ceremony and fun. Perhaps the best example is at Grasmere in the Lake District where the year-long tourist round is interrupted in July by a genuine and not particularly advertised parade of local people who carry rushes and flowers to St Oswald's church, where the poet William Wordsworth and his wife Mary are buried. They pause halfway to sing a hymn, including the lines:

Today we come from farm and fell
Wild flowers and rushes green we twine
We sing the hymn we love so well
And worship at St Oswald's shrine.

Then everyone sets to on a large communal feast, including the local speciality and children's favourite of gingerbread.

Children have always been important in religious village ceremonies as the hope and future of the community, as well as those who will remember the day for longest. Symbolic in the Beating of the Bounds, their presence was welcomed for its natural light-heartedness in another favourite sort of day of fun. These were the topsy-turvy ceremonies associated with Holy Innocents' day – the commemoration of Herod's murder of the firstborn in Palestine – April Fools' Day and the consecration for a single twenty-four-hour stretch of 'boy bishops'. Serving a similar purpose to schools' 'dressing-down days' today, or the licensed mayhem of Red Nose Day, these occasions allowed the community to let off steam by admitting the Lord of Misrule for a brief and very definitely finite moment in charge.

Giving a central role to children was also a practical way of ensuring that misrule did not get seriously out of hand. In France in the fifteenth century special rules had to be passed to limit bawdiness which saw the Magnificat's words reduced to the single line 'He hath put down the mighty from their thrones and exalted the humble and meek' and the clergy procession up the aisle replaced by a donkey, often carrying a prostitute. The new instructions in 1444 acknowledged the tradition of village fun but went into great detail about keeping it within bounds. For example, it said that 'Not more than three buckets of water at most, must be poured over the *Precentor Stultorum* (Bishop of the Fools) at Vespers.'

The only rival to the church's calendar as a governor of village celebrations until very recent times was the changing of the seasons and their demands on farming. Frequently the two coincided and redoubled the jollity at the main festivals, from Christmas through Easter to May Day, Whitsuntide and Harvest, as well as the saint's day of the patron of the parish church. The regular sacraments were also used for activities extending beyond those immediately involved, for instance in the custom of Wedding Races which were held in villages from medieval times until the mid-twentieth century.

These would see one of the main streets cordoned off, usually one with a pub at one or both ends, for locals to tear along to a finishing-line tape held on one side by the bride and on the other by the groom. Relatives of the couple were expected to stump up to help a prize fund which bought the winners gifts such as silk handkerchiefs or wads of tobacco. They would also be invited to the evening party traditionally flung by the newly-weds' parents.

The squirearchy and gentry played a patron's role in these proceedings, usually contributing the most generously to the prizes or allowing their homes and grounds to be used as the destination for races and processions. They would also play a varying part in celebrations which followed important occasions in the farming year, such as 'rent-dinners' after annual leases had been renewed or the wild spending which followed 'mops' and 'statties', the hiring-fairs where farm hands and domestic servants paraded themselves in the village and were taken on for the season, and usually paid their first wage in advance. Sometimes the well-to-do would pitch in over the same plates of beef and pints of beer in their barns or a local pub, but segregation of the classes was also familiar. At Clyro in Radnorshire, the rural researcher Charles Kightly interviewed the daughter of the head gardener at the local hall who peeled the swedes and potatoes for the rent-dinner – twice, because the gentry ate together at the Baskerville Arms on the first evening and their workers on the next.

Behind the gates of the manor house, rectory and other 'big houses' – those of the village doctor, for example, or those characters familiar from Jane Austen who had private incomes and nothing much to do – gentler forms of entertainment were provided. Butts were set up on lawns for archery, a particular favourite among women; and many followed the advice of the gardening writer John James in 1712 when his *Theory and Practice of Gardening* recommended laying out a bowling green:

> *It is one of the most agreeable Compartments of a Garden, and when 'tis rightly-placed, nothing is more pleasant to the Eye. Its hollow Figure covered with a full Carpet of Turf very Smooth and of a lively green, most often encompassed with a Row of tall Trees with Flower bearing shrubs make a delightful composition, besides the Pleasure it affords us of lying along its sloping Banks, in the shade, during the hottest weather.*

Croquet, tennis and clock golf later played a similar role.

Like the priest's use of his garden or the churchyard to host fund-raisers – giving rise to the familiar phrase 'in vicarage if wet' – the big houses often admitted villagers into their private Arcadias for galas, sports and cricket matches on the lawn. Less magnificently but in an impressive show of communal work by people of modest means, village insurance clubs such as the Ancient Shepherds, Foresters and Buffaloes, or 'Buffs', organized Club Feasts to raise money and have fun at the same time. These were marked with almost as much ceremony as the county balls at the big houses; club officials wore green sashes and white gloves and carried staves and banners with Latin mottoes as they processed to the pub or feast field for a hog roast and games – obstacle races for the men, egg-and-spoon for the women. There would be much drinking, except at the otherwise similar occasions mounted by Nonconformist chapels and temperance associations, whose parades included children wearing blue ribbons and singing songs such as:

Water pure, water for me,
The drink of the lion, the brave and the free.

There was much jollity in these, too – the founder of the Band of Hope, Jabez Tunnicliffe, made brilliant use of fun and games – and their races were as keenly contested as those where alcohol was among the rewards.

Races and sporting activities were obvious ways of a small community organizing simple fun and the range of curious examples which survive today shows how inventive villagers could be. The celebrated cheese-rolling carried out at Cooper's Hill in Gloucestershire, which sees bold souls leaping downhill after circular Double Gloucester cheeses whose speed has been recorded at 70mph, dates back 200 years. The coal-carrying race at Gawthorpe in West Yorkshire, now rebranded as the World Coal-carrying Championships, is much more recent but has similar origins as a celebration of an important local product and means of villagers earning their living.

This applied too to the Wagon Day festivals held before the arrival of tractors in many villages where cereal farming was predominant. Carts, wagons and wains would be lavishly decorated with flowers in the week before Midsummer's Day and then harnessed up to take families to the nearest favourite place for a day out. Records of the last Wagon Day to be held at the Yorkshire Wolds village of Rudston in 1919, show that eleven decorated wagons left at 9 a.m. for a trip to the seaside at

Bridlington, two of them marked as 'from Holtbys' – the farm where the novelist Winifred Holtby was working on her early attempts at fiction.

These specific events were fitted in to a round of communal celebrations dating from Saxon times which were known as 'parish ales' because of the beers which were specially brewed for each one, and then consumed in tremendous quantities. An ale could be called at virtually any time, and some were organized specifically to raise funds for wounded veterans of England's many wars, or families in distress. Others, such as the church-ale, were annual events to raise money for church repairs in the way that bazaars and fetes were later to do, but gradually most villages settled down to organizing one big thrash a year, usually at Whitsuntide.

Organized by the church wardens, village ales consisted of an enormous meal laid on for those who bought fund-raising tickets, to go with constantly replenished jugs of the special brew. A flavour of the goings-on is given in Jeaffreson's *A Book About the Clergy* which describes the lengths to which they could go in the mid-nineteenth century:

> *The board, at which everyone received a welcome who could*
> *pay for his entertainment, was loaded with good cheer; and*
> *after the feasters had eaten and drunk to contentment, if not*
> *to excess, they took part in sport on the turf of the churchyard,*
> *or on the sward of the village green. The athletes of the parish*
> *distinguished themselves in wrestling, boxing, quoit throwing;*
> *the children cheered the mummers and the morris dancers; and*

*round a maypole decorated with ribbons, the lads and lasses
plied their nimble feet to the music of the fifes, bagpipes, drums
and fiddles. When they had wearied themselves by exercise, the
revellers returned to the replenished board; and not seldom the
feast, designed to begin and end in a day, was protracted into a
demoralising debauch of a week's or even a month's duration.*

The custom was temporarily banned after the Reformation
because of the sheer excess and the loosening of tongues by
alcohol at a time when the Tudor hold on the throne was by
no means assured. But it has been revived in modern times in
a small number of villages. In Wivenhoe in Essex, the ancient
ale now raises money for St Mary's church, with a decorous
procession of children led by the lord of the manor and his
lady, followed by a hog roast, a medieval mummers' play, riddle
competitions and the chance to learn various ancient crafts such
as making a skipping rope.

The inclusion of riddle-making is a direct throwback to
Anglo-Saxon times when public competitions of clever wordplay
were another village occupation. Although education was
minimal until Elizabethan times, there was plenty of natural
talent among the most humble of the English, and its existence
was recognized higher up the social scale. This is borne out
by stories such as that of Caedmon, the herdsman at Whitby
Abbey in the time of St Hilda, abbess from AD 657 to 680, who
became a noted poet. Many of the riddles also have an earthy
suggestiveness rather than the elegance of learned verbal jokes
which would appeal to educated minds. Dozens of them appear

to refer to sex or sexual organs – references to the object of the riddle sticking out stiffly from a man's breeches, or being offered by a woman to a man so that his head can fill the smallest part. In fact, the answers turn out to be innocuous but clever; in those two examples, a key and a helmet.

These riddles survived for posterity among the limited number of documents or references by slightly later writers which date from the Anglo-Saxon era. By contrast, hundreds of English villages have a large and striking visual reminder of another long-standing entertainment, and one which has kept its appeal into the modern day. The slender maypole, usually painted white and sometimes with red and blue stripes or bands and a carved or metal top, stands on the green or outside a prominent building. Dressed on May Day with red, white and blue ribbons, it forms the centre of complex dancing by pairs of boys and girls, or in villages with a particularly strong tradition, men and women, whose circling patterns gradually interwine the ribbons until they reach to the ground in plaits. The intricacy of the ritual is absorbing and requires a lot of tuition, which is part of its communal appeal in the same way that the oddities of Beating the Bounds were designed to keep the village memory fresh. In Gawthorpe, the home of the coal-carrying race, the maypole ceremonies are both older and more important. Topped with a handsome red cockerel and looped like a candystick with red, white and blue, the village's pole is the centre of major celebrations, including a May Queen competition and a procession of floats, brass bands and dignitaries such the mayor of nearby Wakefield and the local MP.

Far from dwindling into a tourist curiosity, the festivities in Gawthorpe have got ever more sophisticated and notable for community involvement. Since 1906, the local primary school has added six months of tuition in maypole dancing to the national curriculum; its young graduates go on to high school knowing how to trip such plaiting dances as the Barber's Pole, the Centenary Polka and the Spider's Web. The pole itself is regularly replaced at some expense, most recently in 1986 when the previous one, put up in the Coronation year of 1953, was found to be unsafe and about to fall down.

The maypole's appeal as a visible symbol of village fun is reinforced by its parallel tradition of acting as a focus for local pride and resistance to overbearing authority and meddling outsiders. Because of the tradition's supposed origins in the Roman fertility festival of Floralia, when young men stripped branches of their leaves and used them in suggestive displays, church and state have often been wary of licentious goings-on. The gloomy philosopher Thomas Hobbes reacted to the rituals as if they were an early form of pole-dancing, linking them to the phallic Roman deity Priapus, and a national ban was imposed after the English Civil War by the Long Parliament which condemned maypoles as 'a Heathenish vanity, generally abused by superstition and wickedness'.

There has always been some evidence for this, both in records of local smooching after dark on May Day and in books such as John Cleland's 1748 *Memoirs of a Woman of Pleasure* where Fanny Hill makes the obvious comparison as she removes her clients' pants. Sigmund Freud was also convinced of the theory 150 years later. But official disapproval roused the local patriotism of small countryside communities and covert dancing was an important symbol of resistance during Oliver Cromwell's Interregnum. It was welcomed back with hundreds of special ceremonies at the Restoration of King Charles II in 1660.

Nicknamed the 'merry monarch', Charles encouraged the reintroduction of many other rural festivals and was particularly fond of those held on Whit Sunday which was his birthday. This gave a great fillip to morris dancing which had arrived in England some 200 years earlier from Spain, where 'Moorish dancing' was invented to celebrate the country's unification in 1492 with the defeat of the Muslim kingdom of Andalusia and the expulsion of many of its people – the Moors – to North Africa. A more rumbustious version of the delicate patterns woven in maypole dancing, morris has become a phenomenon of modern times, especially with its increasing popularity among women. It is so much enjoyed and so well promoted that it can sometimes seem to be *the* great village tradition and Merrie England's main contribution to world folkore. In fact it was one of a gallimaufry of similar entertainments, including sword-dancing, mummers' plays and guising masquerades, the precursors of Mischief Night in northern England and trick-or-treat at Hallowe'en.

Morris often plays a part on May Day and the fierce protectiveness of villagers over both their poles and the ceremonies is also shown by the tradition of maypole guarding and theft by rival villages, which continues to this day. Beautiful Burnsall, on a loop of the river Wharfe in the Yorkshire Dales, is always alert in late April for stealthy invaders from the neighbouring hamlet of Thorpe, while Barwick-in-Elmet, just to the east of Leeds, has a long tradition of protecting its magnificent pole – at 86 feet one of the tallest in the country – from jealous rivals in Aberford. Gawthorpe again distinguished itself in this side of the maypole's history when marauders from Chickenley tried to remove the 70-foot pole newly donated by a local member of the gentry in 1850. There was a pitched battle after the gang managed to saw halfway through which resulted in one death and one man suffering lifelong crippling injuries before the village's distraught women and children intervened. High winds blew the damaged pole over shortly afterwards. It was all a far cry from today's society, which in 2005 saw a woman from Eastbourne attempt to win £150,000 in damages from the Royal British Legion after she broke her leg in a hole left by a temporary maypole in the nearby village of East Dean. She won the first hearing but the decision was reversed two years later, to national approval, by the Court of Appeal.

The scale of this violent episode is a reminder of the crude nature of village life for many centuries, and the part played in entertainment by proceedings which would be unthinkable today. The stocks which survive on many village greens and are used by visiting children for fun and games, were the centre of cruel bullying as crowds gathered to pelt wrongdoers with filth and rotting food. Villagers also gathered to watch executions on the gallows and gibbets which survive in many places, either as actual structures or in names such as the very common Gallows Hill. Retribution for crime was an important element in maintaining order at a time when there were no police and its symbols were deliberately made prominent. One of the country's highest stood on the South Downs at a point where it was visible for miles, along with decaying corpses such as those of a husband and his lover who were convicted of pushing his wife into a hornets' nest to die an agonizing death. Its maintenance was the duty of the nearest farm, explicitly written into the tenant's lease. At St John's Chapel in Weardale, a pair of handcuffs were kept on the wall of a cottage during the nineteenth century, convenient for use by members of the Weardale Association for the Prosecution of Felons. Across the Pennines, Millom in Cumbria, which was subject to Scottish incursions until the collapse of the 1745 Stuart rebellion, maintained the right of the local Hudleston family to execute felons themselves, with the enthusiastic support of villagers.

The violence never far from the surface in village celebrations ranges from such gruesome extremes to long-lasting traditions such as bare-knuckle fighting, which had an honoured place at fairs and fetes alongside such sporting challenges as manhunts, where a swift runner with a scent box stood in for the fox, gurning – the skill of twisting your face into extraordinary distortions which is still a speciality of West Cumbria – and trying to climb a greasy pole at least 35 feet high. A good example of violence thinly disguised as sport is the famous Haxey Hood game played by more or less the whole village of Haxey in north Lincolnshire, nowadays cheered on by hundreds of outsiders.

Based on a legend about the local lady of the manor losing

her riding hood in a gale, the game consists mostly of a huge rugby scrum known as the 'sway' attempting to push a leather tube to one of Haxey's four pubs. Even today, participants have sharp elbows and alarming shoving ability. But until the late nineteenth century, the ritual also involved tying a villager dressed as a medieval fool to a tree branch and swinging him over a fire until, half-suffocated by smoke, he was dropped into it and left to scramble away as best he could.

The manly achievements of all these competitions had a final side in sportive village life, when the hero of the Haxey Hood, bare-knuckle boxing or greasy pole would find somewhere discreet to spend time with the village lass, or lasses, who had spent the day admiring his prowess. One of the minor pleasures of exploring English villagers is compiling a list of places known for amorous trysts during times when public affection was strictly regulated and penalties could be severe. Lovers Lane is by far the most frequent, but other road names indicate the corner of a village where a blind eye might be turned, especially on high days and holidays. Mabgate is one, with overtones of prostitution, Tickle Alley another and the pretty backwater of Eskdale Green in the Lake District has the appealing Giggle Alley. Appropriately, it is a quiet dead-end leading into deep and sheltering woods.

JOLLY
WAGGONERS

CHAPTER FIVE

TILL AND TITHE

O fortunatos nimium, sua si bona norint, Agricolas!
'O farmers excessively fortunate, if only they
recognized their blessings!'
VIRGIL (PUBLIUS VERGILIUS MARO; 70–19 BC)

Farming and its service trades were the only way to make a living when the Anglo-Saxons set the pattern of England's countryside, and it has been predominant throughout village history ever since. Employment on the land has tumbled to a record low, so that even in one of the country's most agricultural – and beautiful – counties, North Yorkshire, it has been overtaken in the last decade by the number of people who work in the voluntary, charitable sector alone. But the output of a much more efficient system than ever before is still the greatest contribution of the countryside to the national economy, and even more so to that of rural communities.

Farming has had to be productive from the start. In addition to providing for himself and his family, the Anglo-Saxon farmer was bound tightly by demanding obligations to his local tribe, kingdom and church. The rhyming phrase of 'earls and churls' is a simplification but nonetheless denotes the basic structure of society before the Norman Conquest, and one which the Normans were happy to adapt into the feudal system's contract between baron and serfs. A churl, carl or ceorl was usually a free man and the tiny population of a large island meant that he and his family could farm generous plots of land, usually a 30-acre virgate even in the more constricted conditions imposed by the Conquest. But in return, he had a long and complicated list of dues.

In the parish of Tiddenham in Gloucestershire, the 21 hides (an average 120 acres) of land tenanted by such small-scale farmers, alongside 9 hides which were the exclusive property of the local earl or lord of the manor, provided for the community together with a flourishing fishing industry in the rivers Wye and Severn. All rare fishes and every other fish caught had to be surrendered to the lord of the manor and each farmer had to plough half-an-acre of the lord's land every week plus an acre for the church. He had to sow these plots as well, providing the seed for the church himself and organizing his own transport of the lord's seed from the manorial barns. He was also required to provide material for building weirs with fish traps, long stretches of field fencing and to maintain part of the embankment which surrounded the lord's demesne. Reaping and mowing duties in summer came on top of this, along with the payment of sixpence and jars of honey to the lord at Easter, supplies of malt for brewing at Lammas in early August and a ball of yarn for fishnets at Martinmas in mid-November. Finally there were tributes required annually of hens, barley and lambs, and for anyone with over seven pigs, every tenth one had to be given to the lord's household.

This was not a one-way contract, however. By far the most

important gift of the earl to his small farmers was protection and such security as could be guaranteed in a society almost permanently threatened by invasion. Additionally, when the peasant farmer in Tiddenham was given his landholding, he also received two oxen and a cow, six sheep, 7 of his 30 acres already sown, farming equipment and furniture for his house. The humblest members of the village, with holdings of 5 acres or fewer, got additional concessions including waiving of all rent.

Concern for fair dealing between villagers, albeit with the advantage mostly on the lord's side until very recent times, was balanced by a deep-seated awareness of the importance of the land and domestic animals and the need to sustain both. Threats to the environment as we know them today were non-existent, but disease and ignorance were far more prevalent and laws relating to villages and farming took account of this. Even in the case of that diminutive creature the bee, the Saxons inherited from their Celtic predecessors a reverence for its use in making honey, wax and other products. In the laws of the Welsh Celtic king Hywel Dda (the Good) of AD 950, the bee was given special protection and a valuation which traced its origins to the gardens in Paradise. Even greater protection was afforded to cats whose crucial role was to keep grain stores free of rats, and thus potentially save villagers from starvation in the winter months.

Hywel's code went into detail on the merits of a well-bred cat: 'It should be perfect of ear, perfect of eye, perfect of teeth, perfect of claw, without marks of fire, and it should kill mice, and not devour its kittens, and should not go caterwauling every new moon.' Cats appear on carved stones and in medieval monastic illuminated scripts and would have a keeper in more prosperous Saxon villages, probably the same official who looked after the lord of the manor's hunting hounds. A village beekeeper was also a familiar office-holder and his work was likewise much valued.

Codified further by the Normans, the Saxon system of village agriculture proved remarkably long-lasting while at the same time open to innovation when opportunities arose. One example was the cultivation of medicinal plants under the influence of monastic gardens whose keepers benefited from contact with their counterparts on the Continent and were often well-educated men. The English herbal expanded rapidly after 1066 and was quick to include plants such as rhubarb and liquorice when they became available, in both cases more for medicinal use than as a regular part of the diet. In the same way, flowering garden plants which we grow today almost exclusively for ornamentation, were of more interest for their potential as cures.

Major change came only slowly, as the country gradually realized its slumbering power as a wool producer, with perfect pasturing for sheep and abundant clean and swift-running rivers for treatment of fleeces and powering water-mills, whose initial coupling to primitive machinery developed into small factories, first in the Cotswolds and then in northern England. The key was enclosure of communal fields farmed in strips and their conversion into pasture for sheep. The monasteries began it but their dissolution in the 1530s saw it take off, as described in Chapter One. The effect on the national economy was revolutionary and progressive; but successive enclosures meant ruin for the simple peasant farming based on subsistence acreages of cereal crops and small-scale livestock. Although much deplored and opposed, the enclosure movement developed unstoppably from unprincipled Tudor land-grabs to which the authorities turned a blind eye, to the institutionalized division of almost all remaining common land by Parliament at the end of the eighteenth century.

The result at village level was a sharp tilt from a community of many equals, presided over by a small elite but guaranteeing a sufficiency for themselves, to a much less happy mass of dependent labourers working for a prosperous tier of large farms. Social disaster was avoided because, in what has come to be known as the 'English manner', the change took place relatively slowly and the elite were ready to make concessions *in extremis*. There was also recognition on both sides of the skills which long experience had brought to farmworkers whose families had been in the same occupation for generations.

This can be seen in the adjustment by both employer and employee to the shocks which came with the ending of the old certainties of working year in, year out, for the lord of the manor. Its replacement with contract labour and the annual hiring fairs, which some saw as unpleasantly similar to the slave auctions which other Englishmen were holding at the time on their overseas estates, was eased by close relationships between hirer and hired. During his or her guaranteed year of employment, the farmworker would commonly work side by side in field and barn with his employer, share meals with his family, and receive supplements to his payment in kind – chickens, loaves and the like. Although slumps in local economies led to workers travelling about to find work, they were more likely to know their employers. The son of a good shepherd would benefit from his father's reputation; a young woman taken on to clean and bake had a flying start if her mother had a name for both skills.

This was not to last, except in pockets. The nature of the capitalist economy meant that large farms were under pressure to grow larger. Farmworkers began to face stricter, cash-only contracts which included neither board nor lodging and ran for ever shorter periods. Monthly contracts became normal and at busy times such as harvest, farmers started to take workers on for a pittance, throwing them on to the arthritic system of parish relief as soon as their services ceased to add to the business's profit. This destruction of old village bonds and the frightening sense of insecurity which came with it fuelled regular countryside riots in the late eighteenth century, when a succession of poor harvests were followed by harsh winters; and in the 1820s before the Great Reform Bill.

Riotous farmworkers were no match for revolutionary economic forces. Unlike two previous occasions in 1350 and 1650 when the population had been within reach of six million but fell back because of disease and lack of resources, in 1750 the same level was reached with a revitalized farming system which could not only feed the country but export produce. Enclosure was only one of three reforms which made this possible. The second was the invention of farming machinery starting with Jethro Tull's mechanical seed drill, followed by vastly improved iron ploughs and in 1786 Andrew Meikle's threshing machine.

The third was crop rotation, first a three- and then a four-field system of alternating varied plantings and fallow years to allow different nutritious elements to recover and fertility to increase. Promoted by experts including Lord 'Turnip' Townsend who tirelessly promoted the root vegetable as central to the process, this sent output soaring from some 19 bushels of wheat per acre in 1720 to 30 by 1840.

Memorial to the Tolpuddle Martyrs, Dorset

In human terms, however, it sent thousands of newly surplus country people packing to the towns, completed the enclosures' destruction of medieval village ties, and triggered a slow and hard-fought fight for farmworkers' rights. The Captain Swing riots in the countryside of south-eastern England in 1830 showed not only anger at worsening conditions but also a realization of where best to hit back: at the employers' pockets. The frightening part of the outbreak to the gentry and political establishment was less the rioting – of which England has a very long, violent and often successful tradition – than menacing letters from the anonymous mastermind 'Captain Swing' with threats of arson of barns and hayricks which were usually followed up. The protesters were also learning the skills of 'combination', the genesis of trade unions and cooperative societies, which led to a national scandal over the Tolpuddle Martyrs in 1834.

Combining was seen as a threat by employers every bit as clearly as it was recognized as an instrument of reform by workers, especially after the repeal in 1825 of old Combination Acts which had banned any organized attempt at improved working conditions, as opposed to individual negotiation. In 1832 in the little Dorset village of Tolpuddle, six villagers set up a Friendly Society for Agricultural Labourers, led by a Methodist local preacher and requiring members to refuse work offered at less than 10 shillings a week (£45 at today's values). This was volatile even in the remote and largely sleepy county because average wages locally had come down to 7 shillings (£30 today), partly as farmers sought to increase profits and partly because of a labour surplus as machinery began to take up more.

His mind still full of Captain Swing, a local landowner wrote to the Prime Minister, Lord Melbourne, demanding action and a dusty but unrepealed law of 1797 was used to transport the six 'martyrs' to Australia after they were convicted of 'swearing a secret oath' to start their brotherhood. There was national outrage and more than 800,000 people signed a petition demanding their release, as newspapers and pamphlets published and republished these lines scrawled on a piece of paper by the Methodist preacher George Loveless:

> *God is our guide! from field, from wave,*
> *From plough, from anvil, and from loom;*
> *We come, our country's rights to save,*
> *And speak a tyrant faction's doom:*
> *We raise the watch-word: Liberty!*
> *We will, we will, we will be free!*

And four of them soon were, returning to a hero's welcome at the Mayflower Steps in Plymouth, where their radical predecessors had set sail 200 years earlier to found a freer society in North America. But the conditions for which their Friendly Society was founded proved much harder to bring about.

The United Kingdom and her farming were increasingly in the grip of international economic forces, through both competition from other countries and the flow of cheap goods from the British Empire. The convulsions which machinery had brought to the factory system were making new inroads into agriculture too. As well as burning barns and hayricks, Captain Swing had specialized like Ned Ludd before him in wrecking threshing machines and other early automation which was putting unskilled labourers out of work. His gangs' attempts to halt progress were as unsuccessful as the Luddites'.

In some parts of the country, masters and men made reasonable accommodation, but where margins were low or large farms had organized an almost factory-like system of their own to increase production and profits, conditions grew grimmer as the nineteenth century progressed. Harvests rose and money flowed in, but successive governments, influenced by gradual political reform, were concerned. They organized inquiries into farmworkers' conditions not long after the much better-known investigations into factory abuse.

Fifteen years after Lord Shaftesbury's famous campaign which led to the Factory Acts of 1847 and 1853, a Commission on the Employment of Children, Young Persons and Women in Agriculture was despatched by Parliament into the fields. Its findings revealed a pattern of exploitation from the pea-pickers of Norfolk to cocklers on the Dee estuary – interestingly places where ruthless exploitation by middlemen again led to legislation early in our own century, after the tragedy which saw twenty-three Chinese cockle pickers drown in Morecambe Bay. The Commission's list of tasks done by children, usually for a meagre fraction of women's pay which was itself half of men's, started with coppice work in January and ended with stone-picking, spreading cow droppings, and topping and tailing turnips in December. There were at least three jobs for every month between and often more, all of them outdoors in all weathers, lengthy and hard.

The Commission was especially shocked by gang-working – again the central feature of the Morecambe Bay disaster and related scandals in crop-picking areas which emerged in the furore after 2004. Their report described the gangmaster organizers with contempt, referring to the number who were 'indolent, drunken and of a depraved character'. Evidence gathered often described children as young as six slaving away in the fields with none of the dreamy harvest-home atmosphere evoked in the descriptions of rural life some seventy years later by writers such as Laurie Lee or H. E. Bates. In the Lincolnshire village of Ruckland one commissioner found young women so drenched by having to weed in high, wet corn that they took off their dresses and petticoats to wring them dry. Many had rheumatism and one sufferer, still young but a weeder since the age of eleven, told the commissioner: 'We have had to take off shoes and pour the water out, and then the man would say: "Now then, go in again."' Needs must. Like an extreme form of today's two-income households which allow families to cope with mortgage payments and rising prices, farmworkers' households needed a wage from everyone in the family except the very youngest children, to make ends meet.

The weeders were victims of the worst in farming at the time and there was plenty better, not only in the amicable relations between good employers and good workers described elsewhere in this book, but thanks to wider concern about decent standards. The United Kingdom regarded itself as a Christian country and made a lot of 'freeborn Englishmen', British bulldogs and other icons of liberty. A different and distinctly Victorian sort of reformer came into the villages at the same time as the Government commissioners; clergymen and others with a moral mission.

They were especially exercised about young women and saw the entire structure of rural life as designed to subvert their morals and distract them from their 'proper' duty of bringing up soundly prepared children in a clean and tidy home. Visiting a very dirty and untidy cottage, the *Saturday Review* newspaper in April 1858 was scandalized by the practice of boys and girls sleeping head to toe in one big bed in the attic. 'This is the first step to the Haymarket,' said the author of an exposé of rural life for London readers familiar with the capital's centres of prostitution. 'The promiscuous herding of children in their immature years is a not infrequent prelude to a life of harlotry.' Such episodes illuminate Jennie Kitteringham's study *Country Girls in 19th Century England*.

Rough work, crude dress and worst of all labouring alongside men were anathema to the social mores of the clergy and distracted them from any more political social reform they might have achieved. The rector of Ingoldisthorpe in Norfolk sounded a familiar note when he wrote in 1858: 'The dress of the women is almost of necessity immodest. When the crops are wet, they tuck up their dresses between the legs, leaving the legs much exposed.' Worse, he continued, 'the long distance from home often renders it necessary that the women should attend to the call of nature, and this they frequently do in the presence of boys, lads and men.'

There were improvements as a result of all this attention, but they were slow and suffered a prolonged setback with the economic slump which began after the first international financial panic on stock markets in 1873. It was so serious that it was known as the Great Depression until the still worse collapse of confidence after 1929. Historians' attention has been directed largely at the effects on industry and the great cities, not surprisingly as some two-thirds of the country's population lived there, but farming was crushed too. The great novels of Thomas Hardy are mostly set at this time and there is a passage in *Tess of the D'Urbervilles* whose similarity to the 1858 Commissioner's report from Ruckland is striking. Tess and her friend Marion spend all day hoeing a field of swedes:

> *They worked on hour after hour, unconscious of the forlorn aspect they bore in the landscape, not thinking of the justice or injustice of their lot . . . to stand working slowly in a field, and feel the creep of rainwater, first in legs and shoulders, then in hips and head, then at back, front and sides, and yet to work on until the leaden light diminishes and marks that the sun is down, demands a distinct modicum of stoicism, even of valour.*

Hardy was also a realistic observer of farmers' long struggle to keep children at work and out of school, a saga which was still rousing national indignation during the First World War. Outraged that twenty counties had been allowed to suspend the Education Act in 1916 to close schools during harvest so that children could replace enlisted men, the economist and historian J. L. Hammond launched a campaign which widened and led to the establishment of the Agricultural Wages Board in 1917. It was the goal for which George Loveless the Tolpuddle Martyr had scribbled, 'We will, we will, we will be free.'

The setting of better wages coincided with the last years of the UK's international might to create a brief halcyon age for the countryside. The growth of private motoring with

Henry Ford's Model T and its rivals from Morris in Oxford and Austin in Birmingham began the process of daytrips and weekends in the countryside by the town-dwelling majority which were to transform the facilities on offer in tearooms, craft workshops, museums and of course village pubs. This encouraged a sentimental approach to everything rural from the ivy-clad manor house to the hollyhocks and cabbages side by side in the cottage garden. That suited farming so long as imperial preference meant that there was still no need for the country to provide enough to feed its growing population. Canada was bulging with wheat.

The two decades before the Second World War, when the siege of the British Isles by bombers and submarines changed everything, were the time of H. E. Bates and Laurie Lee, sunwashed and full of the loveliness of the English countryside which even its most hard-working inhabitants could begin to enjoy. Jennie Kitteringham contrasts her twentieth-century childhood on a dairy farm with that of the young women in the nineteenth century whose plight she catalogued. 'When I was a girl, children did not work on the land; where once people trod and worked, machines did the ploughing and harvesting. We were rulers of all we surveyed and we had spare time to do what we wanted. I had a childhood. The 19th century girls didn't.'

The gentle pace of the growing efficiency which liberated the farmworker from most drudgery was widely noticed, for example when *Country Life* commissioned a writer in the 1920s to record rural change for a series by cycling from Perranporth in Cornwall to Cromer in Norfolk. He was struck by farmers' loyalty to horses and dislike of tractors; if one of the latter went wrong, he wrote, 'their instinct is to leave it to rust beside the hedge'. Owners of farming's extraordinary variety of horse-drawn vehicles, which included the 'moff' or Hermaphrodite which was half a hay wagon and half a cart joined in the middle, persisted with them. In a retrospective book called *The Departed Village* published in the 1960s, the historian R. E. Moreau quoted an elderly farmworker's take on the interwar years: 'People didn't know no different than to just keep jiggeting along; and whatever they were doing, they were interested in. People were more civilised then.'

Colonial imports saw the price of English wheat fall in 1934 to its lowest level since records began in 1646, while one by one the lingering vestiges of old farming ways came slowly to an end. The last ploughs drawn by oxen were retired in 1929 by their owner Major Harding of East Dean (later to be the scene of the great maypole lawsuit) while scything of crops continued in Essex until 1931 along with the daily 'gleaners' bell'. When this rang for the last time in the village of Farnham, it ended a perk going back for more than a century, which allowed farmworkers on low wages to scavenge for spilled grain between 8 a.m. and 6 p.m. on the day after harvest.

The new era supervised by the Agricultural Wages Board also spelt the end of 'horkeys' or harvest suppers provided free by farmers, who now reasoned that there was no justification for such paternalism. The drift to the towns accelerated and newspapers began to publish the first of many thousands of articles which speculated that the future of the English countryside, commercially, was conversion into a vast and beautiful tourist attraction. A notable step along that path seemed to have been taken in 1930, when the country's last commercial growers of woad, a crop dating back to Boudicca and her blue-dyed warriors in the first century AD, closed their business in Boston, Lincolnshire, after losing their final contract for police uniforms to foreign competition.

One element of old and merrie England persisted, however. The hunt and various allied forms of chasing game flourished as they had done for centuries, allowing villagers of all degrees to forget their differences in the pell-mell pursuit of everything from otters to hares, and of course the fox. One of the surprises of the English countryside to the urban visitor is discovering how much of the landscape has been engineered with hunting in mind. The term 'Fox Covert' for small plantations of trees or broken ground is one of the commonest on the Ordnance Survey. In early medieval times, vast tracts of land were jealously guarded by the Crown and nobility for deer-hunting; and as the stories of Robin Hood make abundantly clear, this was not an activity in which Tom, Dick and Harry were encouraged or indeed allowed to take part. But fox-hunting and the pursuit of smaller prey with beagles and other dogs benefited from a stream of pursuers, some on horseback, others on foot.

Reynard the Fox, John Peel, the red coats reminiscent of both the traditional British army uniform and Oliver Cromwell's 'russet-coated captain who knows what he fights for and loves what he knows' – all were resonances which tugged at the heart of country people and were central to village life. When the

1930s slid into war, the hunt too faced potential extinction. So many leading huntsmen were killed or captured in the early, disastrous, fighting in France, that historic kennels faced closure. But Lady Maud Fitzwilliam of Wentworth Woodhouse in South Yorkshire had an answer – a 'flying pack' able to move between different hunting areas swiftly. She had a name ready for it too: the Spitfires, redolent of defiance – and so the chase went on.

CHAPTER SIX

A HAUNT OF GOOD SOULS

*There is nothing which has been yet contrived by man, by which so
much happiness is produced as by a good tavern or inn.*

DR SAMUEL JOHNSON (1709–84)

When King Alfred took up arms against the Danes in the ninth
century AD to protect his Saxon villages, he made a guarantee to
men who would join him, of land, arms, clothing – and ale. The
staple drink of old England was brewed throughout his kingdom
and much-loved; long preferred to the sweet, honey-based mead
of the Celts, or Roman wine.

From the Saxons' first arrival from north Germany, many
villages had their own 'alehouse' or micro-brewery, turning
barley into malt and then simmering it in water until the
transformation from sugar to alcohol was complete. The weak
version known later as 'small beer' was even more widely drunk;
virtually an alternative for many ordinary households to fresh
water, which could not always be trusted even when taken
directly from rivers or gathered from rainfall in butts.

Ale was naturally valued for its stronger qualities, transporting
the drinker away from a hard world into daydreams and desires
which feature in Anglo-Saxon records, poetry and riddles
as prominently as drink has done in almost every culture in
the world. Carved cups of ale are constantly circulated and

refilled in the halls of epic heroes in sagas such as *Beowulf* where drunkenness was close to manliness. The *symbel* ceremony saw toast after toast by warriors gathered in a *beorsele* or beerhall while the ritual 'alecup' was passed round.

In spite of this macho tradition, much of the brewing was actually done by women, who had their children to mind and the house to keep while the men were out in the fields or away on campaigns. The term 'brewsters' was coined for their job, a now-outmoded feminine form of brewer, just as 'baxter' is for baker and 'spinster' for spinner. When her ale was ready, a brewster would hoist a bush or branch in leaf outside her house and the locals would pile in. This is the oldest of several origins of the common pub name, The Green Tree.

The brewster's kitchen room or proper alehouse became a natural centre of gossip and social gatherings, a role which the country pub still plays in virtuoso fashion today. Usually benign and benefiting the community, the mixture of drinkers and drink could also turn violent, or in the unsettled days of the Saxons, potentially subversive. In 965 King Edgar was prompted by growing disorder to issue a decree that no village should have more than one alehouse.

There was naturally tension over this sort of intervention by the authorities, partly on the typically village grounds of resenting outside snoopers, but also because substandard brews were widespread. The brewster's simple equipment could easily be hidden in the everyday muddle of village farms, and this must account for the surprisingly small number of forty-three breweries recorded in the Domesday Book. Saxon and Norman penalties for brewing ale which was either bad or weaker than claimed, were both severe; in Chester, an offender faced a ducking – a hideous ordeal which sometimes led to drowning – or a 4-shilling fine.

It is scarcely possible to imagine or recreate these ancient precursors of today's country pub today, but certain features of the intimate 'drinking room', with no bar and the brewster fetching jugs of her ale from a barrel round the back, do survive vestigially in parts of the countryside. Somerset still has cider pubs in a scattering of villages where much the same procedures are carried out, with the cloudy and immensely strong drink loosening the tongues of old regulars sprawled in a variety of chairs which have seen better days. The furniture and atmosphere are similar at a proper pub with a bar in the hamlet of Spout House halfway down Bilsdale amid the glories of the North York Moors National Park. Much of the landscape looks as wild as it would have done in Anglo-Saxon times and although the Sun Inn – invariably known as the Spout – is an unlovely Victorian box, the Ainsley family have created over three generations an almost uniquely old-fashioned atmosphere inside. If the barman on duty is having his sandwiches in the kitchen, you are likely to have to wait, not made to feel unwelcome but learning a lesson in patience on utility chairs at Formica-topped tables which came from a Naafi canteen at one of the military bases on the Plain of York.

The Saxons loved games of all kinds and the ancient atmosphere of the Spout is enhanced by its extraordinary cricket pitch whose wicket was long ago cut flat but has an outfield slanting at a ridiculous angle behind the pub, with an ancient iron grass-roller teetering on the slope. For all the challenges posed by this set-up, fixtures are regularly held and on several occasions passers-by have spotted a carroty-haired young player and remarked on his resemblance to Prince Harry. It was indeed the prince, who has regularly turned out for Lord Mexborough's XI in Bilsdale's annual Toffs v Locals derby. Last time, he was clean-bowled by Peter Thompson, a twelve-year-old regular in the Locals' side. Madge Ainsley's underwear billowing from the pub's washing line has acted as a sightscreen in the past, and after games and before returning to the Mexborough estate at Hawnby, the Toffs join everyone else for packed lunch at the Sun. They take their own food, for this is one of England's last remaining 'wet pubs' which doesn't do meals or even snacks. As in an Anglo-Saxon alehouse, you go there to drink. The final element in a lovely ensemble of traces from the past is the Old Sun Inn, just across the courtyard from the Spout and far more picturesque as a structure, if sanitized inside in its modern role as a museum. Its cruck frame dates back more than 300 years and it is full of eighteenth- and nineteenth-century associations with the Bilsdale Hunt; but it is the atmosphere back at the 'new' Sun which seems much older.

Ale remained England's universal drink after the Norman Conquest and at the top end became a drink of some sophistication. Even at court, French wine was sidelined while brewers strove to produce new and interesting varieties of the standard product, much like modern cocktail fixers and with a similar eye on special occasions. When Thomas à Becket went on a diplomatic mission to gain favours from France in 1158, his sweeteners included two wagons loaded with barrels of fine ale. They went down well with his hosts. In his omniscient *A History of Ale and Beer*, H. L. Monckton quotes the chronicler attending the expedition as finding that the French 'wondered at such an invention, a drink most wholesome, clear of old dregs, rivalling water in colour and surpassing it flavour'.

Additives used by these master-brewers included honey and a herbal of plants including yarrow, bog myrtle and ground ivy, which was nicknamed alehoof. Most of them grew wild near villages and gradually became the subject of experiments by the brewsters, whose homely activity could reach impressive levels of production. In Elizabethan times, William Harrison boasted in his book *A Description of England* that his wife and her two maids had an output of 50 pints a day.

That was more than a family was going to get through, however sottish, but it was literally small beer compared to another great stimulus to the development of pubs on a more sophisticated scale than alehouses. Alongside their vegetable gardens and farms, the monasteries brewed ale in heroic quantities; Fountains Abbey in North Yorkshire had an output of 60 barrels every ten days, or some 1,700 pints a day, and that was of proper 'strong ale'. The monks also produced the weaker 'small beer' in quantities large enough to provide their daily allowance of 8 pints each. It sounds a formidable amount of tippling but the alcohol was so weak that vespers were seldom slurred.

The picturesque Bingley Arms in the village of Bardsey-cum-

Rigton between Leeds and Wetherby is testament to monastic and clerical influences which helped it to earn its title as the oldest pub in England.

The Bingley Arms, Bardsey-cum-Rigton, West Yorkshire

There are a number of contenders but the Bingley Arms satisfied the *Guinness Book of Records* with its own records, which describe how one Samson Ellis was brewing ale in the building in AD 953. Not long after, there are references to the pub being known as the Priests Inn, through patronage by clergy from the the part-Saxon church of All Hallows which stands opposite, with the village pillory also nearby, providing entertainment for drinkers after a few pints from Samson Ellis's successors. Under the Normans, the pub became a resting place for monks travelling between Kirkstall Abbey in Leeds, Fountains and St Mary's Abbey in York, and they were noted topers. Not far away, the Ferry Inn at Cawood near York has a record of the Great Feast of 1465 to celebrate the elevation of the hugely wealthy George Neville as Archbishop of York. To wash down meat and pies from 1,000 sheep, 500 deer and 100 cattle, more than 600,000 pints of beer were laid on.

Without the advantages of a clerical connection, later medieval pubs continued to face a difficult task because of the sheer scale of domestic ale production. When the 252 taxpayers of Faversham in Kent were surveyed in 1327, the list included eighty-four brewsters or 'ale-wives' who scarcely left space for a commercial operation. Progress came only gradually, helped by increasingly careful regulation of brewing to avoid not only cheating but serious health problems including fatal poisoning by off-ale. Monckton describes the work of a new sidekick to the shire reeve, or sheriff, who administered the rules of the daily round. This was the 'ale-conner', or inspector, whose pleasant job was to sample village brews. One of his tests was said to be spilling his drink and then sitting in it for half an hour before getting up to see if his leather breeches had stuck to the bench or not. If they had, the ale was too sugary with its fermentation into alcohol incomplete.

Two major developments were to transform the village pub, however, coinciding with the restless years of the Tudor revolution whose effects on farming through enclosure we have already seen. The first was the challenge to ale by beer, two names for drink which are now often used interchangeably, but were distinctly different then. Beer involved the use of hops which the Romans had grown in Britain but as herbs and vegetables and not for brewing. This transformed ale's flavour and body and also helped to clarify the drink and give it the head which has been a passion for many serious drinkers ever since. Its significance was hailed years later in a couplet which went:

Hops, Reformation, turkeys and beer
Came into England all in one year.

It was more like a century, with the first references to beer's incursions in the 1420s, but the sense of major changes throughout society was accurate, and they were felt especially keenly in the small and settled community of the village.

Like most changes to English life, the new drink was regarded with suspicion. Among the 1420s records was a charge of adulterating ale against a brewer who had only added hops, and there were dark accusations about its foreign origins, particularly in what are now Holland and Belgium. Magistrates in Shrewsbury condemned hops as 'a wild and pernicious weed' and a handbook of 1542 called *A Dietary of Health* by Andrew Boorde said of beer: 'It doth make a man fat and inflate the bely, as it doth appear by the Dutch men's faces.'

The trouble for ale partisans was that many of their fellow countrymen had been over to fight alongside those Dutchmen in Flanders and had developed a liking for their beer. It was a better, tastier and more nutritious product and its triumph could never seriously have been in doubt. With it came greater complications in manufacture and this encouraged larger and better-regulated breweries at the same time as the countryside began to see the division of alehouses into two different types: the inn and the pub. The inn catered for travellers and still today is often marked by a very high arch to allow loaded carts and later stagecoaches through into the yard and stables at the back. The pub developed the old alehouse role as a social centre for the community, often giving space to other activities such as the Forest of Bowland's Swainmote Court which heard poaching and timber theft offences at the Hark to Bounty in Slaidburn in Lancashire. This was interestingly similar to today's spate of extra uses for pubs in villages which have lost facilities such as post offices and shops, banks and even churches. The Newton in Sprotborough in South Yorkshire hosts a mass on Sunday mornings because there is no Catholic church. Once established, the country pub very soon began to adopt features which have distinguished it ever since.

The Crooked Chimney, Lemsford, Hertfordshire

Prominent among these are the signs which famously hang or stand outside the pubs, from a dozen or more called the Good, or sometimes Silent, Woman (with no head and therefore no tongue) to the Crooked Chimney in the Hertfordshire village of Lemsford whose inspiration is there for all to see. Tipping a cap to the Anglo-Saxon love of riddles, other names derive from puns or mishearings, such as the Bag o' Nails which comes from the ancient Greek drinking ceremony of Bacchanals.

These jokes and curiosities were a sidebar to the more serious role of early signs in gaining respectability for a pub by attaching it to authority via a large and public declaration of loyalty. There was no bigger advertising space in the late medieval or Elizabethan village than the pub signs. It is no coincidence that the seven most popular names of UK pubs are all expressions of support for royalty: the Red Lion, a badge used by the Scottish incomer James I after Queen Elizabeth's death; the Crown; the Royal Oak recording Charles II's hiding in a tree after the battle of Worcester in 1651; the Rose and Crown; the King's Head; the White Hart, badge of Richard II; and the Queen's Head – although traditional waggishness converted one of these, in Brighton, to show the late Freddie Mercury, lead singer of the band Queen.

In the same manner, pub names such as the Bear and Staff and the Talbot used the coats of arms of noble families – in those cases the Earls of Warwick and Shrewsbury – while hundreds of village pubs sought favour with the local big family by using their name followed by 'Arms', as the Bingley Arms above. In some cases, the tribute was not genuinely voluntary but an instruction of the family itself, which would usually be the landlord until the expansion of large breweries into pub chain ownership in the nineteenth century. The huge popularity of the Red Lion, with over 600 pubs carrying the name, and of the White Hart which is not far behind, have similar origins. James I made it an instruction that public premises should stick up pictures or models of his lion as he travelled south from Edinburgh to London. Richard II was the monarch who first decreed that all pubs should have a sign, and his badge was adopted so universally during his reign that White Hart became a synonym for 'pub'.

Indoors, most country pubs adopted another division which has lasted until the present although the growth of fine dining and admission of children have made inroads into the distinctions. The public bar was the home of locals, often including regulars who would claim their customary chair or place on the bench and order their drink simply as 'the usual'. The price of beer was usually slightly lower and the decoration sparse – well summed-up as a 'symphony in brown' by historian and philosopher Lewis Mumford and memorably described by Richard Boston in his excellent book *Beer and Skittles* as having the 'austerity, control and simplicity usually associated with Japanese design'. That, and the depth of a patina on the tables which can only come from hundreds of years of spilt beer, and nicotine stains which make walls above the dado rail look like a vast smoker's fingernail. The saloon bar or snug is contrastingly cosy and plush, cluttered and ready to receive the lord of the manor or a hunting party or the regulars' wives, should they call by.

A fancy saloon bar may still boast small bells in the wall, a feature inserted once electricity had arrived to summon bar staff who were usually within normal earshot anyway. In place of these, the public bar offers another marvel of the country pub: a range of games which can while away an evening even when conversation lapses, and also help to pace the progress through pints of a customer who doesn't want to get blind drunk. Darts is the foremost of these, a game which is as interesting to watch as to play. It grew in fashion after rowdier entertainments were banned, including the various forms of animal fighting which gave their names to pubs such as the Cock or the Dog and Duck. It was far from the countryside, but my home city of Leeds played an important part in the legalization of darts when the city authorities tried to have it banned in public places as a game of chance and therefore gambling. A noted player called Foot Annakin who ran a pub in one of the city's twenty-six 'alphabet streets' – now sadly demolished, they stood in a line off Kirkstall Road from Aleph to Zennor Street – was summoned to court and subjected to an experiment by the magistrates. Playing against the court clerk, who had no experience, he threw three 20s followed by three treble 20s. The clerk missed the board altogether. There was only one possible verdict and this urban drama saved the 'arrows' in thousands of country pubs.

Dominoes is next in popularity, originally from the Far East but popularized by French prisoners-of-war in Napoleon's time, followed by cribbage, the only card game exempted from the Gaming Act provided the stakes are token, Nine Men's Morris, bar billiards, bar skittles and shove ha'penny, a game which initially seems to be stultifying boring (you just do what its title suggests) but turns out to be fascinating, full of tactics and very illuminating on the power range of the human hand, fingers and thumb. In larger pubs or outside in yards, skittle alleys are firm favourites, sometimes alongside Crown Green Bowling. One of the most enjoyable misunderstandings I ever witnessed was when the alley at the Windsor Castle pub in Bath caught fire and an older reporter colleague, who was forever pointing out our mistakes, rang the press office at Buckingham Palace to ask increasingly angrily why so little was being divulged about the fire at Windsor.

Inns meanwhile developed into the marvellous, rambling collections of building which give such joy to tourists today, with creaking stairs leading off at all angles, plumbing which carries the detritus down the plug of one bath and up the overflow of another, haunted rooms and vast fireplaces where a whole family can sit on the fender and still not block the warmth from spreading to others around the room. The severing of ties between Britain and her rebellious colony the United States lasted long enough for the word to become a universal synonym among Americans for 'hotel'. Holiday Inns are perhaps the best known usage, just as the Inns of Court in London derive their name from the inns where out-of-town barristers would stay.

Running an inn was usually a profitable business in itself although dangerously vulnerable to changes in transport, such as the coming of the canals and railways, which might divert its trade; or the moving of a market from one town to another. Country pubs could be more fragile financially unless the village was large and reasonably prosperous. The unusual-sounding Bhurtpore Inn at Aston in Cheshire, named after the last great rebel fort in British India which was captured by the local landowner General Lord Combermere, was an example. The family who took it on in 1849 found that it would not pay on its own, so bought a network of fields around the village to supplement their living with farming and also added a small brewery. Pub names such as the Blacksmith's Arms at Swinton in North Yorkshire and the Cobbler's at Pontefract came from secondary occupations of past landlords. At Paull on the Humber estuary, the landlord of the Humber Tavern earned £2 a month (£180 at today's values) from Trinity House for use of a powerful lamp in one of the upper rooms as a temporary lighthouse in 1836 until a permanent tower could be built.

Beer's steady popularity as the lifeblood of old England took on new impetus in the late eighteenth century when the Dutch were responsible for introducing a genuinely damaging drinking habit in the form of gin. It swept the households of the poor, as the quickest means to temporary oblivion, and the dreadful social consequences were most famously portrayed by Hogarth in his engraving of *Gin Lane* (1751). Less well known today is its opposite, *Beer Street*, which showed none of the depravity rampant in Gin Lane but portrayed cheerful and industrious John Bulls, laughing as they flirt with pretty girls. Its accompanying poem by Revd James Townley, whose verses on Gin Lane denounce the 'cursed Fiend, damned Cup', reads:

Beer! Happy produce of our Isle
Can sinewy Strength impart
And wearied with Fatigue and Toil
Can cheer each manly heart.

Labour and Art upheld by Thee
Successfully advance
We quaff Thy balmy juice with glee
And water leave to France.

Encomiums such as this preserved beer's elevated status as a kind of national elixir well into the nineteenth century and even the early temperance campaigners were cautious about condemning 'small beer' when the alternative was increasingly polluted water. The evils of spirits, especially gin, dominated public policy and the Beer Act of 1830 actually encouraged the opening of 'beer houses' in private homes; almost a return to the days of the Saxon brewsters, with minimal infrastructure and beer sold from the front window or door. Within a decade, there were more than 45,000 across the country and Britain was awash with cheap drink very much in the way brought about by supermarkets today. The authorities realized two things: beer was not entirely harmless, especially when sold dirt cheap and in vast quantities; and the number of outlets was threatening the livelihood of traditional inns and pubs.

The big brewers, which by now had thousands of tied houses in both town and countryside, applied pressure for more regulation, in an unlikely alliance with temperance campaigners.

The brewers wanted a tougher regime for the beer houses while the teetotal reformers set up 'dry' alternatives to pubs known as British Workmen's Public Houses. When the White Swan in Chapel Allerton, then on the outskirts of Leeds, lost its licence in 1867 because of violence, it became a 'British Workmen's', selling such calm-inducing products as Winterine, Anti-Burton and aerated milk, non-alcoholic alternatives for wine, beer and champagne. Its sign appealed:

A Public House without a drink
Where men may read and smoke and think
Then sober home return;
A stepping stone this house you'll find
Come leave your rum and beer behind
And truer pleasures learn.

So began the long march of licensing, up the hill from the first limits imposed under the Wine and Beerhouse Act of 1869 and then down again from a peak of restrictive measures in the 1914 Defence of the Realm Act, a dramatic name for a bill which dealt with all sorts of social matters including rationing and censorship, but scooped up pub opening hours among them. It reduced drinking time to a draconian 12–2.30 p.m. and 6.30–9.30 p.m. Pubs in the munition-making area of Carlisle were nationalized so that moderation could be enforced directly by the state.

This led to the countryside tradition of the lock-in, the closing of tucked-away country pubs on the evening deadline, but with regulars still inside for what then legally constituted a private party. This was taken to greater although legally dubious lengths in places such as Lindisfarne or Holy Island in Northumberland, where pubs could relax once the tidal causeway was flooded and, provided no constabulary were staying or had got stranded, stay open for the next eight hours.

As the twentieth century rolled on, and the long saga of disputes and inefficiencies in farming were gradually resolved, the country pub also entered a new and prosperous stage. Higher incomes and all-but-universal car travel transformed the old sandwich and ham-and-eggs menus, rooms with en suites became familiar features. More and more pubs turned into inns. But there was more to come to their story, both in terms of disaster and triumph as we will discover in due course.

CHAPTER SEVEN

MAKING AND MILLING

History has remembered the kings and warriors, because they destroyed; art has remembered the people, because they created.

WILLIAM MORRIS (1834–96)

It is easy from a modern perspective to look back on the long and intimate history of the English village and farming, and to conclude that everyone in the countryside must have worked in animal husbandry, cereal crop-growing or both. But this overlooks the huge number of skills related to farming which developed as separate ways of earning a living, and in more recent times, the establishment in the countryside of businesses employing many people which have nothing to do with agriculture at all.

Diversification began early on, but always in a way so subordinate to the annual harvest or the seasons of breeding, rearing and slaughter that it could be difficult to discern as a separate occupation. The mill was one obviously distinct operation, requiring the miller to have detailed knowledge of machinery which was sophisticated by the standards of the time and also dangerous. He needed experience, too, of the best techniques for grinding different grains to make flour. A smithy also became an essential and clearly specialized part of most Anglo-Saxon villages. The story of Wayland the master smith, who made the great hero Beowulf's armour, was a favourite at feasts and other gatherings, and a blacksmith's role in forging and sharpening weapons for both the battlefield and the hunt, and later shoeing horses, made him an important figure.

Within early medieval households, other skills developed out of necessity. Butchery was essential to cope with the 'cottager's friend', the unfortunate pig who for centuries would be fussed over for much of the year and then slaughtered in bloody circumstances which many a country child has recounted in graphic memoirs. This was famously a feature of many homes during the Second World War when possession of the single pig allowed under emergency regulations, and the careful slicing and preservation of its many parts after slaughter, added immeasurably to the rations. Memories again provide much evidence of this, along with more ominous official documents about the lavish scale of contraband. Shropshire's archives describe incidents of secret stairways hiding second or third pigs, flitches of salted bacon being stashed in babies' cribs, and the stalking and eventual prosecution of a farmer near Shrewsbury who was notorious for supplying black market pork. His cache of carcasses was found hidden down a disused well.

The war's enormous increase in home husbandry in the countryside, with allotment numbers leaping from 815,000 in 1939 to 1,400,000 four years later and the Domestic Poultry Keepers' Council recording a record 1,250,000 members by 1945, also mirrored life in Anglo-Saxon and Norman times. For English men and women in the 1940s, these measures were the result of a temporary emergency. During the millennium of the medieval period, from AD 400 to 1400, they were the stuff of daily life. Along with butchery and animal husbandry came skills at bee-keeping, wildfowling, and crafts such as joinery and a huge range of textiles. Fishing also stimulated a wide range of subsidiary ways of earning a living: the making and improvement of rods, nets, fish-traps and small river boats such as coracles. A speciality of Wales and the Welsh borders, coracle-making continues to this day, adhering to the principle that the willow rod shell with its tarred skin of hide or calico must be light enough for someone to carry on their back. A coracle proved its seaworthiness in 1974 by crossing the English Channel, and the best-known maker of modern times, the late Fred Davies of Shrewsbury, used to pootle about in his little walnut-shell on the river Severn during Shrewsbury Town FC football matches, retrieving any balls kicked out of the nearby ground.

If a cottage could thus become a miniature factory, the productivity and innovation of monasteries established after the Norman Conquest brought large-scale manufacturing to the countryside. Buried in the woods around the Leeds suburb of Horsforth is one of the country's oldest bloomeries, or furnaces for smelting iron. It was built by the monks of Kirkstall Abbey, founded two miles down the river Aire in 1152, who also managed a large brickworks and acres of gardens, with plots for vegetable growing and a physic section for medicinal herbs. Further into the Dales, the monks at Jervaulx Abbey brought in high-quality sheep from the Continent and southern England, crossing them with hardy Pennine stock to create famous breeds such as the 'Swardal' or Swaledale. They began the enclosure movement some 200 years before it became notorious, creating larger pastures but never on a scale which aroused serious enmity from villagers whose strip-systems were sacrificed. The lost land included formerly Celtic lynchets, irregular-shaped strips contoured into the hillside like South Asian rice paddies, whose remains can still be seen all over the Pennines, especially when sunny weather casts shadows from the different levels. Again, the villagers were not unwilling to sacrifice these to the abbey in return for a share of its growing produce and technical help with their own small-scale agriculture from the monks. The greatest legacy of Jervaulx's many innovations was the famous and distinctive Wensleydale cheese.

Cheese-making, butter churning and the production of relishes, compotes and jams whose modern successors line the shelves of every rural craft outlet in England today, have also been staple, small-scale 'industries' in villages for centuries. They could be made by the women and children at home, in the tradition of beer's brewsters, and this also applied to cottage textiles: spinning, weaving, and – in parts of the Midlands, especially round Leicester – shoe- and glove-making whose specialists were spared from too much rough work at home or in the fields because they needed pliant and delicate hands. An interesting consequence of the countryside's development of glove-making skills was the employment of women from villages round Oxford at William Morris's car-making plant in Cowley during the first half of the twentieth century. Selecting, cutting and sewing the leather trim – hard parts of the hide for seat bottoms to cope with heavy wear, softer cuts for the flexible door-opening loops – were similar to the skills learned with gloves.

The former Cistercian abbey of Rievaulx, near Helmsley, North Yorkshire

The monasteries again developed such techniques on a larger scale and a major community such as Rievaulx Abbey on the edge of the North York Moors was not so different from a late eighteenth-century northern town at the beginning of the Industrial Revolution. It is hard to imagine in the abbey's exceptionally beautiful and tranquil little valley today, but before its dissolution by Henry VIII, Rievaulx's economy was based on 24 square kilometres (9.2 square miles) of land with 12,000 sheep, and smoke belching from some of England's biggest iron smelters. One of them was capable of exceptionally high temperatures through the power of a large waterwheel and the monks mastered a system not only of bloomeries like Kirkstall's, to produce 'blooms' or red-hot lumps of spongy iron, but also string hearths where impurities were driven out of the blooms in an early form of refinement. Another waterwheel powered a large hammer to improve the string hearth's work and in the last days of the monks, output reached over 40 tons of iron a year. Such an asset was too useful to crumble into picturesque ruin, as happened to the abbey's religious buildings, and local Tudor entrepreneurs kept things going. They rebuilt the forges in 1576 and converted them into a blast furnace which produced 100 tons of pig iron in its first year. This rose to 280 tons by 1624 and the furnace lasted until 1647, when the disorder of the Civil War and the rise of Britain's first large-scale heavy industry in the Black Country of the Midlands meant that the balance sheets no longer added up.

Feeding the furnaces stimulated another rural industry through the voracious demand for charcoal, which led to the coppicing of more than 20 acres of nearby woodland. Across the moors, meanwhile, a string of coastal villages were profiting from large-scale quarries and cliff-mines for the alum trade. Like the graphite of Borrowdale in the Lake District, the presence of alum-bearing rocks and particularly the techniques involved in breaking them down into alum powder, were closely guarded secrets. Invaluable for treating leather, fixing clothing dyes and a range of medicinal uses, alum's chemical compound comes from heating appropriate rocks in a furnace and then treating them with mineral water and exposure to the air until the soft, white powder spills out. This was little understood in Tudor England, but in the late 1590s a member of Yorkshire's new rich who had profited from the dissolution of the monasteries, Sir Thomas Chaloner, managed to smuggle two skilled workers from the Pope's closely guarded alum works near Rome where processes were the best in Europe. Bringing them back to England, allegedly hidden in a barrel for some of the time, he established a hugely successful alum industry between Scarborough and the Tees, which continues today. One of the deepest mines in Europe at Boulby now reaches far below the sea to produce half the UK's output of potash as well as tonnes of rock salt as a by-product. Just as Chaloner was, it is a major employer of modern villagers, and has also inherited his sparky imagination. Chaloner used Londoners' urine as ballast in his ships returning from taking alum to the capital, after finding that the liquid was excellent for the mineral water stage of the chemical's refining process. Equally brightly, Cleveland Potash at Boulby persuaded scientists searching for that elusive substance dark matter, whose existence has been proved in theory but not yet in fact, to house their main European laboratory down the mine.

Blast furnaces and alum were at the dramatic end of the scale of specialized trades which absorbed villagers all the year round by the nineteenth century, and were to an extent a cushion against the vagaries of unstable farming markets and erratic harvests. In her study of *Country Girls in 19th Century England*, the historian Jennie Kitteringham makes her way through every imaginable skill from basket-making in areas rich with osiers such as the Somerset Levels and along the rivers Trent and Thames, to braiding fishing nets, cutting rags for hop manure, stripping bark for tanneries, making lace in the Midlands, stacking turf in Staffordshire and puddling clay at brickworks everywhere to crush out lumps. Most of these had roles for women and children and in the plait-making trade, which churned out hatbands, decorations and lengths of beautifully intertwined straw with names such as pearl, bird's-eye and whipcord, the whole family was involved in the most literal sense. The London *Morning Chronicle*'s survey of rural life in 1850 found children as young as two involved in the simple but arduous process. Much like essentially bogus classrooms used in some Third World countries today as covers for child labour, village 'plaiting schools' were set up for these mites by women experienced in the trade. Until the Education Act of 1870 they would usually intersperse a lot of plaiting with a little Bible-reading and the occasional hymn.

England's copious woodlands provided another wide range of tasks, as detailed by Thomas Hardy in *The Woodlanders* (1887), whose sturdy heroine Marty South turned her hand to weaving wattle, making chairs out of fine beechwood, brushes from less valuable trees, and besoms when she had a spare moment. Besoms in particular were a favourite product for wood scavengers and the 1869 National Commission into the work done in the countryside by women, young people and children, found no fewer than fifteen families earning a living from making the 'witch's broom' brushes in and around the Nottinghamshire village of Farnsfield. Carving wooden toys was a village speciality, much-revived in rural craft workshops today. And another of Marty's skills, in coppiced areas of woodlands used for charcoal like Rievaulx Abbey's, was splitting hazel branches to make spars for thatched roofs.

Thatching itself was of course a major village business. It gave rise to a number of familiar English surnames, not only 'Thatcher' which politics has made famous but also 'Maslin', the term for the mixture of wheat and rye which were the standard material for rural – and many urban – roofs from Anglo-Saxon times. Thatch has come back into fashion in the modern era and the UK now has more than 1,000 people employed in a craft which in the 1950s was considered doomed; but much of the material is imported and since the coming of the combine harvester in the 1920s, it has been hard to envisage the long, stout stems of local straw which made such an effective covering in the past.

In medieval England, wheat regularly grew to over 6 feet and its straw was as carefully cut, kept and dried as the grain. Thatchers would then apply it in layers to roofs, using the hazel spars split by the likes of Marty South to fix each new covering on top of the old. Among some 250 houses in England whose thatch dates back for over 500 years, there is ample evidence of how effective the covering was. Well-applied, a thatch could last up to fifty years before needing a fresh layer, although the depredations of rain, wind and nesting birds usually made renewal on humble farm cottages a more frequent chore.

The effect is extremely picturesque and a major contributor to the cosy feeling of the English village. Combined with the handiness of cheap local material and skilled thatchers within reach of every home, the roofs were popular well after the railways made slate from expanding quarries and mines in Wales and the Lake District widely available in the nineteenth century. It was only with the additional revolution on road transport and the improvement in everything from mains electricity to plumbing which came in the twentieth century, that thatch was seen as a sign of backwardness and poverty. And that stigma was short-lived.

Another attractive village roofing which made use of local material was pantiling, whose use remains almost universal in areas such as North and East Yorkshire where clay is ample and the ports convenient for ships from Holland and Belgium where tiles have always been produced in large quantities. The S-shape of the interlocking tiles had been widely used by the Romans, including in Britain, and proved an effective way of sluicing off the rain. Pantiles were also lighter than the heavy stone slates familiar in more inland parts of the north and more easily replaceable when they slipped or cracked. They remain a bright and appealing feature of England's eastern coastal areas today, just as the stone slates have also survived and indeed become as sought-after as thatch. The old medieval ploy of turning stone slates over when their tops become worn is also an ancient custom which has been revived, often with startling effect. After years of exposure to the weather, the stone develops the dark colouring familiar from illustrations in books such as *Wuthering Heights*. Its underside, snugly protected among the rafters, usually remains the original honey colour, and thus a 'newly turned' roof completely transforms a building's appearance.

The use of local materials for building makes for one of the most fascinating aspects of the English countryside, as buildings change shape and colour depending on the dominant stone – dark or reddish grit, luminous limestone or the intriguing magpie effect of a mixture of the two in areas such as the Craven Fault in the Yorkshire Dales where buildings and especially drystone walls are like chequerboards because of the use of both types of stone. Bricks, too, come in a spectacular range of colours from the mellow brown of Old London Stock to Reigate Purples and the somewhat lavatorial appearance of Cambridgeshire White. The name 'Brickfields' is common in English villages in areas where clay predominates and small-scale enterprises were run by families until the end of the nineteenth century. The children were responsible for the puddling, making a soft and consistent paste by repeatedly treading the clay – a job done by herds of cattle and sheep on the beds of canals and village ponds whose clay liners are usually remarkably impervious as a result. The paste would then be moulded into bricks by the adults and fired in a communal kiln; or in successful small enterprises, the family one, which would be kept well away from any thatch. Although as fireproof as most other roofing materials, straw roofs are almost certain to be totally destroyed if flames do take hold.

In *Country Girls in 19th Century England*, Jennie Kitteringham traces an account of family work in a brickfield at Iver, Buckinghamshire, in 1903 to the County Record Office in Essex, where the writer moved after marriage. Called *My First Job*, it describes the arduous routine for a young girl, especially when diverted from puddling to loading her father's moulded bricks on to a barrow, sanding them before firing and then wheeling them across the yard to another worker who would take them to the kiln. The work started at 6 a.m. and ended at 6 p.m. with three half-hour meal breaks. Pay was 9 shillings a week (£40 today), of which the girl kept sixpence (£2.20).

Another fine example of geology's effect on building styles is the use of flint in East Anglia, with church towers distinctly rounded to accommodate the uneven stones and beautiful patterning on walls to show off the bluish outside shades in contrast with the shiny, oyster-like scoop inside each nodule. The art critic Kenneth Clark, later Lord Clark, was entranced by the effect, writing of Suffolk's masterpieces:

> *The use of this magical material reaches a high point at Butley Priory and Gipping, where flint work is used with the precision of the inlaid marbles of the Taj Mahal. In the famous Priory gatehouse, flints produce a rich, precious texture, unique in the architecture of the world.*

His praise would no doubt have delighted the anonymous village craftsmen responsible, and perhaps astonished them with its lavish opinion of what at the time would have seemed a straightforward and practical use of local stone. Flints have an obliging habit for builders (although not for ploughmen) of working their way to the surface, but in East Anglia men had dug down for larger quantities since early prehistoric times. The remarkable bellpits of Grimes Graves in Norfolk, rediscovered in the 1870s, were full of worn deer antlers used between 8000 and 2000 BC to carve through the chalk to the rich layer of flints below. The scale of the quarrying was such that archaeologists reckon 25,000 stags were killed to provide the implements discovered.

Prehistoric man was after weapons and tools as much as building material, and this aspect of flint was another important local industry, with centres almost as concentrated as the Borrowdale graphite mine, which was given a royal guard of soldiers in Elizabethan times as the country's only source of a vital ingredient in advanced gunpowder. The village, later town, of Brandon in Norfolk developed a name for very high quality 'black flint' originally used for 'strike-a-lights' – the predecessors of matches which raised a shower of sparks when struck against iron. This soon developed into musket flints for the army. Brandon became a byword for the best of these in the eighteenth century, knapped (or shaped) with skills which became subtler when local men served overseas and picked up techniques from French prisoners. In the 1821 census, Brandon's population of 1,770 was made up of 353 families of whom 137 were sustained by trade and manufacture including flint, compared to only 20 dependent on farming.

Although there were many fewer people working on farms in the mid-nineteenth century than 100 years earlier, output grew steadily thanks to the range of new agricultural machines. These were too large to be made in villages but their many associated products and constant need for repairs could be handled locally. Blacksmiths diversified to run workshops which resembled the small garages still commonly found in villages. Sadlers and oastlers grew used to cutting and sewing belts for the broken drives of threshing machines and later traction engines and early tractors. This new work drew on a very old tradition of making farm implements which needed craftsmen highly skilled in both joinery and metalwork. To make a scythe, for example, required precise calculation of both the twist of the wooden handle and the setting of the blade, while the medieval mouldboard plough, used for heavy soils where wheeled versions were too weak, had to strike the right balance between heavy-duty size and weight and being mobile enough for oxen to shift. Some of the greatest village skills continued in the production of carts, traps, 'gambo' flat-wagons and haywains, in which I have a natural interest as a Wainwright. Their role in English life was so long-lasting that 'wagon' is still widely used to describe modern lorries in northern England.

Designing their superstructure was more complicated and delicate work than a battered old relic, rotting away in the long grass today, might suggest. When the Barnsley brothers of Birmingham, Sidney and Ernest, set up their communal cottage workshop in 1892 at Sapperton in the Cotswolds, and began to produce superb handmade furniture, they spent much time hunting down humble village techniques to copy. Among these was a process of chamfering, or bevelling edges of wood which both produces an interesting and attractive shape, and – more importantly to the practical cartmaker – cuts down on unnecessary heaviness which might slow down even shire horses. A fine example can be seen at the idyllic village of Owlpen in Gloucestershire, where a large cupboard made by Sidney Barnsley in 1913 acknowledges in its plans and preliminary drawings 'motifs as used by the wainwright, where the chamfers reduce weight'. The Barnsleys were very much part of John Ruskin and William Morris's belief in the nobility and purity of rural crafts, and the sentimental shape of things to come in the English countryside was shown in their long contract to design and furnish Rodmarton Manor, also in Gloucestershire. This vast and glorious fake is an early twentieth-century pastiche of a sixteenth-century manor house; Disney in many ways, but in terms of craftsmanship, Disney to the highest possible standards.

The Arts and Crafts-style Rodmarton Manor, Gloucestershire

We have dwelt at length on beer in the previous chapter. There was another famous drink, however, which was even more connected with the countryside: cider-making. The famous firm of Bulmer's started in the Herefordshire village of Credenhill where the rector's wife advised her unemployed sons to start a food or drink business 'because these things do not go out of fashion'. The advice had the same good sense as Mark Twain's dictum which underlies the centuries-long success of the English gentry: 'Buy land. They're not making it any more.' Edward and Percy Bulmer duly started with two casks of perry, alcoholic pear juice, using a stone-mill operated by a pony at a neighbouring farm, which gradually crushed the sweet fruit in a circular trough. The business grew to international fame, and in the process brought work to hundreds of country people in a great diversity of trades. Apples need growing, picking, conveying and pressing before the magic of creating the finished drink to a particular recipe, with all the fermenting and other processes involved. Cider even had a role as part of village workers' wages until such in-kind deals became illegal when the Truck Acts were extended to agriculture after the First World War.

Farm cider-making appeared to have died out by the 1950s, with major companies such as Bulmer's dominating the industry, but in common with many other old village trades, it is returning on a modest scale. Today's new rural world of well over a thousand trades, from telecottaging to the supply of oversize bras by Ample Bosom on a farm at Old Byland in North Yorkshire, may soon see the ancient cider tradition of cellar-whistling revived. This was devised by farmers who stashed their best casks in the cellar but found them empty the following Christmas, often with neat cork-sized holes bored by farmworkers or housemaids who had gradually helped themselves. Whistling was therefore required by anyone who went into the cellar, to show – unless there was a telltale gurgle – that they could not be drinking at the same time.

CHAPTER EIGHT

THE ENGLISHMAN'S HOME

The palace is not safe when the cottage is not happy.
BENJAMIN DISRAELI, FIRST EARL OF BEACONSFIELD (1804–81)

The English country cottage is one of the most delectable creations of mankind, both in the idea which plays on so many imaginations across the world, and in its reality – at least today. It has long been common ground among historians and sociologists that the cosily rounded walls, ancient beams and twining roses often hid a slum as bad as any in the more obviously bleak industrial towns. Even when disease and squalor ruled indoors, the effect of so many different styles over so many years, seldom with any conscious planning, gave an effect from outside which was defiantly picturesque. In the eighteenth and nineteenth centuries, wealthy landowners indulged a fad for what was called the *cottage orne*, a theatrical attempt to provide their workers with little fairy-tale homes. What was the point? The real village was as *orne* as the most demanding lover of beauty could wish.

Village cottages were humble, the homes of the least wealthy, but they have come to hold more appeal for many visitors than the grander buildings which are their neighbours – the Queen Anne rectory, the Georgian hall or the medieval church renovated by Sir George Gilbert Scott. All these fall into categories which, although immensely varied to the expert eye, easily seem samey to the casual visitor. Another triangular pediment supported by more columns? Another set of rooms filled with gold-framed family portraits and rural views? Been there, done that, probably got the T-shirt too.

Cottages on Gold Hill in Shaftesbury, Dorset

But cottages tumble this way and that, stagger downhill in streetscapes such as Gold Hill in Shaftesbury, meander along the river in Lower Slaughter or Castle Combe, huddle together against the felltop wind in Middlesmoor at the head of Nidderdale. No window is straight, no wall without a bulge, comfortably like the one in the midriff of many of the sightseers who these days come pottering round. Materials are so local that the buildings can seem to grow out of the ground, the pinkish-brown earth in the garden transmuting naturally into the pink-washed daub on the walls between the supporting beams. Heavy thatch sags like a tow-head of hair on a Saxon child. Gardens which have adopted the name of 'cottage' to represent a particularly lovely mixture of flowers and vegetables in apparently carefree muddles, surround the buildings on all sides.

It is easy to get carried away, isn't it? But there are logical reasons for the beautiful lack of logic in most English villages, or at least the absence of formal planning except where an entire community has been uprooted and rehoused to meet the demands of a mansion with a Capability Brown, Kent or Repton view. Very few have suffered from catastrophes which have led to large numbers of homes being replaced at the same time – and when that does happen, its unusual nature makes the result all the more glaring. A drive to build council houses in villages in the 1950s was socially very welcome but carried out clumsily, leaving effects which are starting to mellow but still need much more time. You can see this in an otherwise outstandingly pretty composition like Chapel Stile in the sensational surroundings of Langdale in the Lake District. A curve of houses provided by the local authority are of excellent quality and essential to the flourishing of a healthy community. But their numbers and similarity are at odds with the appealing jumble all around.

But if the layout of villages we see today is usually very ancient, the actual houses are less so. Americans often say modestly that their 'new' country inevitably lacks the ancient charms of England, but scarcely any homes of the 'ordinary' English country dweller survive from before 1700, and the Pilgrim Fathers and their descendants had been in Massachusetts and its neighbours for eighty years by then. After a comprehensive survey resulting in the failure to find any pre-1700 housing which could have belonged to villagers below the modestly prosperous yeoman class in the whole of West Yorkshire, the Royal Commission on Historical Monuments concluded in 1986 that 'The vast majority of poorer families must have been housed in buildings incapable of standing the test of time, or not susceptible of the sort of piecemeal improvement which would have warranted their retention.' Even the handful of tiny squatters' homes they discovered failed to make the grade, such as Mizpah Cottage in Bardsey-cum-Rigton, home of the ancient Bingley Arms pub with its Saxon roots. Although simple and single-storey, this bold invasion of the village green lasted long enough unchallenged to claim permanent status, but it was built well into the eighteenth century. You have to travel 30 miles up the river Aire and cross into North Yorkshire to find a similar example from earlier times. The Squatters' House at Airton managed to get through a system used in the early seventeenth century which allowed homeless villagers to apply to the Quarter Sessions for permission to build a house in a village on common land. If they could hold off the usual determined efforts of their potential new neighbours to prevent this, and get the basic framework of a cottage up within twenty-four hours, they could stay. The Squatters' House is rare testimony to the handful who succeeded.

The disappearance of humbler cottages in West Yorkshire happened in a county richly endowed with sandstone as well as ample timber. In parts of the country to the south and west where wattle and daub was the almost inevitable material for the smallest homes, the chances of their lasting until today or forming the core of a later house are slimmer still. Cottages which have survived from before 1700 were a cut above, built by the yeomen whose loosely defined class in late medieval times ranged from prosperous farmers whose descendants were accepted as gentry after the Tudor revolution, to neighbours whose holdings were much smaller but still owned freehold. They were the likely builders of most of the sixty-one ancient cruck cottages found by the Commission in West Yorkshire, as well as others which had been demolished but not before precise records were made of their appearance. These include a cottage close to Bracken Hall in Baildon which was inspected in 1904 by a local antiquary, W. P. Baildon, who had obvious reasons for taking a particular interest. He gives a good description of the appealing simplicity of such buildings:

The rock, which is here covered very thinly with soil, had been bared and levelled and in it were sunk four holes, one at each corner of a square. Four massive oak timbers, shaped something like a boomerang, or a ship's rib inverted, were inserted into the holes, two and two, so that each pair met at the top. These carried the roof tree, which in turn supported the rafters. A wall has been built round, and a fireplace and chimney in the middle completed the cottage. I saw this picturesque and interesting building in 1884; it was pulled down shortly afterwards.

Cruck cottages abound across the British Isles, many of them engulfed by later additions so that only a crawl into the attic or peering behind a wall cupboard gives a clue to the original construction. Such exploration can be a greater revelation than expected. At Shandy Hall in Coxwold, famous as the fictional home of Tristram Shandy and the actual parsonage of his creator Laurence Sterne, restoration work revealed wall paintings dating from Tudor times, some hundred years after the timber-framed building was commissioned in 1430 by a wealthy local landowner, George Dayville. The hall was greatly superior to any ordinary cottage in those days and indeed served as the village manor house, but its compact size and cottagey air of cosiness serve to emphasize how small most pre-eighteenth-century village homes tended to be.

The restored cruck cottage at Torthorwald, near Dumfries

Other fine cruck cottages include one at Torthorwald near

Dumfries which has been lovingly restored and opened as a museum by the Cruck Cottage Heritage Association. Even in its neat and tidy state, however, it shares with the vanished house at Baildon that 'primitive' feel which the antiquarian Baildon noted. Thinking back on its bare rock floor, even when strewn with rushes or covered by straw-plait mats, it is easy to understand a villager's response even as late as in 1909 when interviewed by Miss M. Sloane for her book *An Englishman's Castle*:

> *'Is your father comfortable in the almshouse?' I asked a very respectable, hard-working villager.*
> *'Well, he ought to be, miss. He has a boarded floor.'*

Boarded floors might remain a luxury for cottagers, but the agrarian revolution of the late eighteenth century and the profits to be made from mechanization in the early nineteenth were responsible for many of the pretty village homes we see today. Clearing away the dilapidated hovels which housed many of their labourers, newly prosperous farmers used stone and sound timber for new cottages, while usually following the previous higgledy-piggledy plan, which has become such an endearing characteristic of the English village. The developments stopped short of the *cottage orne* which still wealthier landlords were starting to introduce as lodges or tied estate homes, but they began to pursue an image which national sentiment was encouraging, and was soon to adopt wholesale.

This image was based on the larger and better-built homes

of medieval and Tudor yeomen which still stood in respectable numbers, rather than the original cottage whose very name in the English of the time was a disparaging term. The word derives from Old English, Norse and Old French words all meaning 'hut', and in the country's first attempt at a census, in 1688, the year of the deposition of King James II and the Glorious Revolution which installed the reforming partnership of William and Mary, the humblest 400,000 of the population of 5,500,000 were classified as 'cottagers and paupers'. The many attempts at poor relief during the reign of Elizabeth I, particularly aimed at 'sturdy beggars' and promoting the concept of the deserving and undeserving poor, include an Act against the Erecting and Maintaining of Cottages, in 1589. This required any new cottage to be endowed with four acres of land, a virtual impossibility for anyone but a thriving farmer. Its target was any addition to the existing stock of shacky hovels, which were considered lairs where the undeserving poor could hide.

The rules behind the enhanced cottages begun in the late eighteenth century were summarized by Jane Austen in her delicately satirical way, when Mrs Dashwood visits Barton Cottage in *Sense and Sensibility* (1811) and finds it commodious and well furnished, but 'as a cottage, it was defective, for the building was regular, the roof was tiled, the window shutters were not painted green, nor were the walls covered with honeysuckles'. The unplanned Arcadian look which has become the central motif of the English village cottage today, and for most of the past two centuries, was the crux. What went on behind its picturesque facade was something else again.

Today's beautiful cottages with their prices topping £1 million in favoured counties were an entirely different matter when rooms were crammed with as many as twelve people, sewerage and fresh water were non-existent, and infectious disease, or minor but debilitating skin and other conditions, were widespread. In his excellent study *The Truth about Cottages*, John Woodforde combines the idyllic plans and prospectuses of cottages from 1700 onwards with ruthless dismantling of the notion that the dream was regularly, or indeed possibly ever, made real.

Woodforde quotes the medical officer for Chippenham in Wiltshire on conditions in nearby Colerne, a straggle of pretty cottages on a hilltop above the A4's old coaching road to London which today command breath-taking prices. In the late 1830s, by contrast, the scene was one of filth, dilapidation, squalor and a medical casebook which was never free from smallpox, scarlet fever and typhus. Sentimental paintings of rosy-cheeked maidens at the gates of their cottages, which do indeed tend to have Jane Austen's green-painted shutters and hollyhocks abounding in their gardens, should really be studied with a soundtrack of terminal coughing from a tuberculosis victim indoors, and a scratch-and-sniff facility to release the stink of ordure, rotting food and drains. In the same year that the Chippenham doctor was making no bones about the reality of cottage life, *Punch* published a biting satire of one of the era's favourite bards of the middle classes, Felicia Dorothea Hemans. Where she had written:

The cottage homes of England!
By thousands on her plains
They are smiling o'er the silvery brooks
And around the hamlet fanes

the magazine substituted instead:

The cottage homes of England!
Alas! How strong they smell
There's fever in the cesspool
And sewage in the well.

The theme was taken up by Charles Dickens whose account of a brickfields hovel in *Bleak House* (1853) combines raw description of the conditions, drawn from his own experience, with ridiculing the absurd Mrs Pardiggle who swans in on her improvement mission oblivious to an infant who actually dies in her presence. She continues to distribute an improving tract which, Dickens says, was so boring that 'he doubted if Robinson Crusoe could have read it, although he had no other on his desolate island'. None of the brickworkers huddled in the filth could read anyway, although the father of the household gives Mrs Pardiggle a broadside on the foul bucket of slop which his daughter is using for a wash, the stink of gin and the fact that five other infants have preceded the latest to the grave.

Woodforde goes so far as to suggest that tumbledown cottages and waif-like children were considered to be 'desirable ornaments of the countryside' for the watercolour brushes or poetry jotters of Jane Austen's idle young ladies. That is going a bit far, but it is noticeable how Pardigglish moral concern almost vies with straightforward descriptions of squalor in nineteenth-century official inquiries. Like the clergy who bemoaned the bare legs of young women who took off their petticoats when weeding rain-drenched wheatfields, the Report on the Sanitary Condition of the Labouring Classes ordered by the Home Secretary in 1842 dwelt at length on the dangers of young boys and girls sharing bedrooms within a family, or the impropriety of a teenage lad flinging his nightshirt off in front of women in the household, to get a better wash.

The strength of the criticism had little direct effect on the countryside's landlords, at least initially, but it prompted a series of manuals on how to build a cheap but decent country cottage which gradually caught the attention of at least some of the gentry. Their interest was encouraged from the throne itself, with Prince Albert exhibiting designs for a block of four model cottages at the Great Exhibition in 1851 and then building fifty-eight examples with Queen Victoria's encouragement on the royal estate at Windsor. As Woodforde notes, the Prince's involvement is a useful reminder that squalor in the mid-nineteenth century was not a blight on the poor alone. The typhus which killed Albert, just as it did the villagers of Colerne, is thought to have come from leaking cesspools serving the outmoded plumbing of Windsor Castle.

Designing the perfect cottage became a mark of the entire nineteenth century and continued well into the twentieth. From its foundation in 1842, *Builder* magazine published blueprints for small homes, influenced like Prince Albert by the botanist and gardening expert John Claudius Loudon's majestic *Encyclopaedia of Cottage, Farm and Villa Architecture* (1833). This incorporated knowledgeable detailing, such as large windows to allow tailors or cobblers to conduct their work in decently light conditions at home, and sewage tanks where waste could be stored until in an acceptable state to be used to fertilize the garden.

Matters gradually improved, with fresh air and outdoor work helping farmworkers' health and resistance to disease, and the encouragement of small vegetable plots, pigsties and paddocks where space allowed. Even in the eighteenth century, foreign visitors had commented on how the English cottagers' diet was usually better than those of peasants in their own countries. Most had meat twice a week as well as bacon and other pork products from their pig or pigs, bread, milk, cheese, a mixture of vegetables and, of course, a great deal of beer. The gin-soaked misery of Dickens' brickfield workers was accurate but far from universal. Families who had the energy and persistence to avoid falling behind, in spite of the harsh conditions and absence of all but the crudest social insurance, could cope and sometimes thrive.

The turn of the century and the spread of new building materials brought further reform, as architects and social campaigners challenged a long-standing belief among landowners that 'decent' cottages came too expensive. The Arts and Crafts movement and shortly afterwards the pioneering of 'garden cities' with plenty of modest housing alongside roomy villas, starting at Letchworth in Hertfordshire in 1903, stimulated competitions to produce good quality cottages at low fixed prices. At the cost of a maximum of £150, the proposed new housing allowed a level of rent that gave the owner sufficient return and contingency money for repairs, without crushing the tenants and driving them into debt. In 1914 *Country Life* magazine lowered the bar to £125, which was met by a successful pair of three-bedroomed semis whose materials included reinforced concrete.

The battle was essentially won by the 1920s, but as late as 1944 Winston Churchill's Government commissioned plans for 'emergency cottages', capable of very rapid construction, to house an expected flood of demobbed servicemen and -women back to the countryside after the end of the war. The chosen design's cost of £1,000 was considered profligate and, worse, to suffer from a return of the sentimentalism of eighteenth-century attitudes to the cottage ideal. The Women's Institutes of Northamptonshire organized a competition to come up with alternatives which attracted 500 entries. The organizers emphasized the importance of the practical as opposed to ideal, commenting:

> *It is a false assumption that the average rural worker welcomes an almost all-glass south wall. He spends his whole day out of doors and when he returns home, he wants, first, somewhere to put his bicycle away, then a WC, somewhere to remove dirty boots and wet clothes and clean himself before entering the house proper. There he would like to find a fire doing an efficient job economically.*

For all these years, as huts and hovels grew gradually into cottages and primitive facilities were slowly improved by sanitation and extra space, the cottage garden played an important part in both the appearance and the economy of the little homes. Its origins lie, like so much of the history of English villages, in Anglo-Saxon times, with the growing of useful plants for the household close to the front door. England before the Norman Conquest had many links with continental Europe and the knowledge of herbs and vegetables was regularly refreshed by visitors and trade from France, Italy and Spain. The handful of Anglo-Saxon herbals which have survived were translated from Latin texts. Their origins are obvious in paintings of scorpions, which were not a feature of England's wildlife, and varieties of plants such as henbane which were natives of the Mediterranean, not northern Europe.

The monasteries, especially those of the vegetarian Benedictines, gave gardening lore and practice a major stimulus, although Norman herbals continued to illustrate both plants and animals which would never be found in the British Isles or, in the case of a large blue elephant in Eton College's copy of a treatise by the Roman Apuleius, anywhere in the world. Villagers would be lucky to see such material or to understand it if they did, but the Elizabethan chronicler Raphael Holinshed recorded plenty of practical, kitchen garden experience in times past. He wrote in 1577: 'Such herbs, roots and fruits as grow yearly out of the ground have been very plentiful since the time of the first Edward,' and lamented that during the Wars of the Roses and the reign of the first Tudor monarch, Henry VII, they had become neglected 'so that they became unknown or supposed as food more meet for hogs and savage beasts than mankind'.

The long period of disorder in the late medieval era was certainly a setback to progress which, historians now believe, was probably given a hand by another disaster, the Black Death plague of the fourteenth century. The loss of over a quarter of England's population gave extra room in villages for cultivation. Once the Tudors had settled in, this revived, with extra stimulus from the daring overseas voyages of sailors and explorers such as Sir Walter Raleigh and Sir Francis Drake. New and better herbals encouraged the pace, especially the famous *Herball or Generall Historie of Plantes* published by John Gerard in 1597. It was targeted at grand gardeners as well as lowly ones, with an appropriately florid dedication to Lord Burleigh which began:

What greater delight is there than to behold the earth apparelled with plants, as with a robe of embroidered worke, set with oriental pearles, and garnished with great diversitie of rare and costly jewels?

The old herbal weaknesses of muddle and confusion remained rife, however, with Gerard describing in detail, albeit only from hearsay as he admitted, a non-existent barnacle tree which produced shells instead of fruit. He also located the potato's country of origin as Chile rather than North America.

New plants including such modern staples as the potato and another American discovery, the tomato, further encouraged cottage gardeners, but a reaction set in against attempting anything approaching Gerard's metaphor of a lavishly decorated dress. Rather, commentators began to emphasize the virtues of the unplanned mixture of flowers and vegetables which came to encapsulate the phrase 'cottage garden'. The mixture was the merit: marigolds offered not only their vivid orange for beauty but also added colour to butter and cheese and zest to soup. Most of the standard cottage annuals, such as pansies and mignonette, had medicinal uses. The same applied to the great perennials: cowslips, foxglove, hollyhocks, lavender, lily of the valley and sweet williams. Other plants provided dye colours and there was usually a score of herbs for cooking and medicine, led by the famous quartet of parsley, sage, rosemary and thyme.

One of the greatest poems ever written on the subject, Andrew Marvell's *The Garden* composed in the 1660s, does full justice to this mixture in the exultant lines:

What wondrous life is this I lead!
Ripe apples drop about my head;
The luscious clusters of the vine
Upon my mouth do crush their wine;
The nectarine and curious peach
Into my hands themselves do reach;
Stumbling on melons as I pass,
Insnared with flowers, I fall on grass.

Alexander Pope, too, wrote in 1713 in favour of gardens with the 'amiable simplicity of unadorned nature' and by the end of the following century the triumph of the genre was complete.

The great and prolific garden writer William Robinson filled his masterpiece *The English Flower Garden* (1883) with illustrations of cottages smothered in hollyhocks, rambling roses and dozens of other rampant flowers and observed: 'One lesson of these little gardens, that are so pretty, is that one can get good effects from simple materials.' His book is highly enjoyable for its trenchant headings: Evils of Bedding and Carpet Gardening (the opposite of cottage gardens' riot of different flowers, with plants and turf marched into fixed beds like military units); Misuse of the Yew Tree; Against Useless Stonework; Monotony; and The Evil Effect of Books on Italian Gardens. The cottage garden has never faced serious criticism since.

CHAPTER NINE

GHOSTS AND GRIME

Old farmhouses with their white faces
Fly, and their ghosts have taken their places
Even the signposts like grim liars
Point to the trapping brakes and briars.
EDMUND BLUNDEN (1896–1974)

No conventional English villages were built after the reign of Queen Elizabeth I but there were plenty of curious newcomers, from pit villages flung up by coal companies to religious groups' attempts to found Utopias on earth. There were also regular additions to the sad roll-call of those which have disappeared. The great laureate of these, Oliver Goldsmith, did not write his wistful masterpiece on *The Deserted Village* until 1770, but he was familiar with the slow disappearance of ancient communities from the landscape. The most famous lines from his elegy are as moving as Thomas Gray's recollection of an English country churchyard which General Wolfe recited as his troops prepared to storm the Heights of Abraham and seize Quebec from the French.

Ill fares the land, to hastening ills a prey,
Where wealth accumulates, and men decay;
Princes and lords may flourish, or may fade;

A breath can break them, as a breath has made.
But a bold peasantry, their country's pride,
When once destroyed, can never be supplied.

The romantic poem has a yearning effect when recited amid the overgrown relics of long-gone villages such as Pudding Norton, Godwick or Little Bittering, three of 110 lost communities in the county of Norfolk. Plague, enclosures, repeatedly failed harvests or just a gradual inability to sustain a hamlet on poor or insufficient land, did for them all and more than 2,000 elsewhere in England. In some cases, a lonely church amid fields is a reminder of the bustling life which once went on around. In others, only mounds are left.

Godwick, near Fakenham, was an example of devastation by the Black Death which left only ten households scratching a living by 1428, attrition which continued through a succession of harsh winters and stunted crops on the unforgiving clay soil. In 1525, the number of taxpayers was down to five and the last rooms were emptied and doors closed for ever before the end of the century. Meanwhile, other Norfolk villages fell victim to enclosure and the invasion of ancient strip farming systems by grazing sheep. Among the victims were Bawsey, Leziate, Mintlyn, Narford and Sturston. A third, man-made means of destruction was the legal practice of engrossment which enabled a lord of the manor to revoke tenancies and repurchase the freehold of land after cottagers died. Gradually this removed the means of making a living for all but the manor estate itself. It did for Threxton and West Raynham and played a part in the disappearance of Narford.

In other places, it was nature which drove the villagers out, sometimes dramatically as with the coastal erosion which has seen forty towns and villages disappear into the sea between Bridlington and Spurn Point on the East Yorkshire coast. The sometimes theatrical collapse of villages along with the cliffs inspired the artist equivalents of Goldsmith, notably the painter J. M. W. Turner at Dunwich. Slow erosion has continued the destruction of this Suffolk coastal settlement's churchyard to this day, with leg bones sticking eerily out of the steep cliff in the 1970s and providing a handhold for bold venturers making a risky circuit of the collapsing remains. Little Waxham in Norfolk long ago went the same way, as did Eccles-on-Sea which was washed away in a storm of 1604 with another violent winter finishing off the remains of the church tower 291 years later. At Sidestrand, the church was dismantled before the sea could claim it and most of the materials were used to rebuild it safely inland, but St Peter's, Shipden was not so lucky. It was engulfed in the fourteenth century at the time of the Black Death, but enough of its tower survived underwater to damage a tug which struck it in 1888.

East Anglia's Brecklands saw a different type of erosion, with the unstable sandy soil blowing away like sandstorms in the desert, sometimes loosened further by landowners' digging of warrens to breed rabbits for food. When John Evelyn inspected the area in 1677, he described 'the Travelling Sands that have so damaged the country, rolling from place to place like the Sands in the Deserts of Libya, quite overwhelming some gentlemen's whole estates'. Kenfig on the coast of South Wales, was a similar victim, overcome by sand dunes which had been made unstable by local people digging out the timber and plants which had previously bound the shifting sand together. Hallsands in south Devon collapsed into the sea between 1903 and 1917 after its sea defences had been undermined by the dredging of shingle just offshore.

Tilgarsely and Tunmore are two villages in Oxfordshire known to have been wiped out, every man, woman and child, by the Black Death. To the south-west, the hamlet of Snap in a dry valley on the Wiltshire downs near Aldbourne sustained a population of between forty or fifty, remarkably steadily, for over four centuries. But in the late nineteenth century, changes in agriculture saw the modest balance sheet of the solitary large farm dip irretrievably into the red. Its owners moved out and six of the seven cottages were abandoned soon afterwards. Only an elderly couple remained for a few more years until they too left and the fields and woods reclaimed the little settlement. Other gaps in the patchwork of England's villages were left much later by military requisitioning. Special dispensations to visit are still allowed for church services at the lonely remnants of Imber in the army's vast firing range on Salisbury plain, a closed area since 1943 when villagers were given six weeks to pack up and go. The crumbling houses of Tyneham on the Dorset coast have similar open days when the tanks stop firing, and relatives of the villagers expelled during the Second World War, with a promise of return which was not honoured, are allowed back.

Such places have a special atmosphere and, in the case of the military land, extraordinarily abundant wildlife. Although there may be the occasional threat of live ammunition and shell explosions, the absence of human beings puts Imber, Tyneham and miles of surrounding, empty countryside among the country's very best nature reserves. On the gunnery ranges at Warcop in Cumbria, the shattering of hard ground has encouraged badger setts, deep in the earth beyond the impact of most shells.

The Victorian model village at Saltaire, near Shipley, West Yorkshire

A different distinction surrounds another special kind of village, which appeared in considerable numbers during the Industrial Revolution. Concerned by the squalor of cramped urban slums on their factory doorstep as far too many workers crowded into cramped or hastily jerry-built homes, more mill-owners and other manufacturers than conventional history suggests laid out 'model' villages. These were so well built that most of them not only survive today but are sought-after, expensive homes. Saltaire, which surrounds Sir Titus Salt's mammoth alpaca mill by the river Aire in West Yorkshire, is a handsome grid of streets named after the magnate's family members, with a range of sizes to suit different households and workers' grades of employment. Salt also provided a town hall, institute, chapel, almshouses and hospital, but strictly no pub. Only in recent years has a wine bar opened, opposite the mill whose collection of paintings by David Hockney is the finest in the world. Its name is Don't Tell Titus.

Saltaire is a World Heritage Site and the best-known nineteenth-century industrial village in England, but there are dozens of smaller examples. Just over the Pennine foothills, Halifax has Ackroydon, a smaller square of fine houses built by the carpet manufacturer Colonel Ackroyd, and the small urban village of Westhill Park, laid out by his even wealthier rivals the Crossleys who, most unusually, did not commemorate themselves in their benefaction's name. In Bradford, Ripleyville built by the textile magnate Sir Henry Ripley who made a fortune from the fixative properties of his black dye, no longer remains but is commemorated in both the name of a block of council flats and a mural in their lobby. In the twentieth century, the great Quaker chocolate dynasties of Cadbury and Rowntree built Bournville in Birmingham and New Earswick in York, the latter with a fine Moot Hall designed to encourage community involvement and village democracy. Samuel Whitbread created a little paradise for brewery workers in Southill, Bedfordshire, and Austin imported flat-pack homes from Canada to provide cheap but decent housing for his Longbridge car-makers whose numbers vastly increased during the First World War. He had to do this twice, after the first consignment of timber and metal fixings was torpedoed by a German submarine.

A few model villages were built by country gentry, not as a result of laying out new parks where the old hovels had to be removed from the Arcadian view, but for more altruistic reasons. Among surviving examples are the fine Arts and Crafts cottages commissioned at Snelston near Ashbourne in Derbyshire in 1847 by John Harrison, the squire of Snelston Hall. Harrison employed a high quality architect, Lewis Nockalls Cottingham, who later supervised repairs to Rochester Cathedral and established a Museum of Medieval Art at Waterloo in London, using salvage from demolished buildings. Squire Harrison's motives, helped by possession of a large fortune, were to improve both the conditions of his estate workers and the look of the village in its pretty setting on either side of a winding tributary of the river Dove.

His enthusiasm for the Arts and Crafts movement was shared by a rather more unexpected village-builder, the Bolsover Colliery Company, which laid out a model community for its workers at Creswell, also in Derbyshire, around a spacious village green with a miniature railway supplying the miners and their families with their own pit's coal. Another prominent architect, Percy B. Houfton, carried out the work in 1895 and 'The Model', as locals have always called it, was restored in the 1990s and still provides comfortable and well-appointed homes.

This was not always the case. One of the former GPs who

rented the 'practice house' in the Northumberland colliery village of Murton remembers the wind actually whistling between the bricks of the walls whose cement pointing had never been properly done. In spite of this – and we have already seen the ferocious loyalty of former mining families in County Durham to their 'shacky' villages after the pit closures of the 1950s – workers made good use of communal facilities and built up the neighbourly spirit which lies at the heart of much prettier rural settlements. Such ardour was naturally attractive to writers, and the hugely popular medical dramas of A. J. Cronin such as *The Stars Look Down*, a hit film in 1940, were set in a fictitious pit village called Sleescale which was recreated for the film at St Helen's Siddick colliery near Workington in Cumbria. The cultural tradition continued with *How Green Was My Valley*, the Paul Robeson hit *The Proud Valley* and, in recent times, *Billy Elliot* which was shot on location at Easington Colliery in Northumberland, the next village to Murton, home of the wind-whistling doctors' house.

The work was the thing in such industrial villages, however, and when it ceased, many of them came to an end. Dylife in Powys was a lead-mining community which simply dispersed when falling prices closed the workings in the mid-nineteenth century. Porth-y-Nant on the Lleyn peninsula of North Wales was abandoned when its quarry shut down; and Binnend in Fife lingered on, but only half alive, after the shale works which it was built to support in 1881, closed only thirteen years later. The last few elderly inhabitants left in 1954. Bothwellhaugh on the river Clyde lost its last residents in 1959 when the local Hamilton

Palace colliery closed and the shutting-off of its pumps led to disastrous problems with sewage.

Another well-organized attempt by industry to revolutionize village life was carried out by the British Fisheries Society, the brainchild of a London bookseller with the inspiring name of John Knox, who set up a joint-stock company in 1788 and set about building a new community at Ullapool in Scotland, which took its first residents in 1800. Another thirty-nine fisheries' villages followed around the coast, though not all could cope with the ravages of the sea. The old smuggling port of Hampton-on-Sea on the coast of north Kent was chosen to house an oyster fishing company in the 1860s, complete with a seaside estate of residential housing. Unfortunately, the following three years saw violent storms which eroded the coast unusually swiftly. Only a few houses were built and in a renewed onslaught by the weather the following year, they had to be torn down as the sea swept inland.

Industrialists who laid out these model villages were influenced, in part, by another group of idealistic planners, the religious communities which set up their own villages to preserve common values as well as provide a decent standard of homes. There were a great many of these, from late Tudor Puritans to the pacifist Bruderhof from Germany which settled the Shropshire village of Wheathill during the Second World War with 200 members who were reluctant to join the majority of their compatriots who started a new life in Paraguay. Others included the Alpha Union of the Brotherhood church community on the edge of the pioneering garden city of Letchworth in 1905 and the Canossian Sisters of Charity who briefly established a chapel in the extraordinary village of Dailymail in Hertfordshire, made up of forty-one different houses from the 1922 *Daily Mail* Ideal Home exhibition, surrounded by a belt of equally varied fruit trees. Almost as unusual was the nearby collection of thirty-five plots in woodland rented by nudist families in 1929 for a community inspired by Germanic notions of the healthy body beautiful and known as Spielplatz, or Play Space.

Most of these enterprises were enthusiastic but short-lived. The Moravian settlement and school at Fulneck between Leeds and Bradford is of an entirely different order. Named after the town of Fulnek in the Moravia province of the Czech Republic, it thrives today in a beautiful terrace of Georgian houses complete with a heritage plaque commemorating the architect who built the US Capitol in Washington. This was Benjamin LaTrobe, son of the headmaster of the school, whose distinguished pupils later included the factory reformer Richard Ostler, the Liberal Prime Minister Herbert Asquith, and the actress Diana Rigg. His career exemplified the hard work and self-improvement inculcated by the Moravians, who emerged from remote areas of rural Czechoslovakia in the late seventeenth century, calling themselves the 'hidden' seed of the early Protestant movement led by Jan Hus which had been condemned as heresy by the Roman Catholic Church nearly three centuries earlier. The community was originally intensely inward-looking, with marriage partners initially chosen by lottery on the grounds that all members were equal in virtue (if not in physical appeal, but that was an earthly consideration). Missionary work was by contrast a very outward-looking affair and the Moravians, whose beliefs still flourish in Fulneck, were famous for their work among the world's most downtrodden, including Native Americans at the worst time of persecution by the expanding United States, and slaves on the plantations of the Caribbean.

The Rest House at the model village of Bournville, Birmingham, West Midlands

Similar idealists in the Chartist movement for political reform also created lasting settlements, using their principle of three acres and a cow to set up five villages on neat grid patterns with modest but well-designed houses surrounded by land. Many of these can still be seen at the sites chosen by the Chartist Co-operative Land Society in 1845, which attracted 70,000 subscribers and initially planned to allocate plots by lot. Parliament ruled this illegal and development went ahead on more conventional ownership lines with houses going to those who had paid the largest advance deposits for them. The communities at Heronsgate in Hertfordshire, Great Dodford and Lowbands in Worcestershire, Minster Lovell in Oxfordshire, and Snig's End in Gloucstershire retained a radical spirit for years, concentrating on sustaining their members by their own efforts, or what the Chartist leader Feargus O'Connor called 'blistered hands, fustian jackets and unshorn chins'. Great Dodford was successful as a centre of strawberry growing and, in a nice completion of a virtuous circle, sold its products to the Quaker chocolate makers at nearby Cadbury's, whose workers from the model village of Bournville turned them into strawberry creams. At Heronsgate, which was also known as O'Connorsville just as the Minster Lovell village was called Charterville, a pub retains the idealism in its unique title: The Land of Liberty, Peace and Plenty.

An entirely different way in which new villages were created was in the concept of the 'urban village', a make-believe which has no practical connection with the countryside but tried to draw inspiration from its supposed virtues. Many guides exist to such concepts as the 'Villages of London' and indeed the 'global village' where the homely qualities of olde England's cosy homes are encouraged as a counter to the busy roads, crammed trains and strife of real life. They have more than a touch of William Morris's *News from Nowhere* (1890), which portrays the London suburb of Kensington transformed into a trouble-free version of Sherwood Forest in a medieval England wonderfully free of famine, feudalism and plague. As John Carey writes, in his commentary on an extract from the novel in

The Faber Book of Utopias (2000), the urban village's inhabitants are 'polite, jolly, friendly people with musical laughter and prettily embroidered clothes. They love folk festivals, handicrafts and hay-making. The women are lightly clad and affectionate and enjoy waiting on, and cooking for, the men.'

If these idealistic notions of a village within a city are insubstantial, one of the strangest of English villages ever built was anything but. In 2004, a surveyor from a development company on the north-west border of England, Nick Paxman, stood in a wooded glade on the edge of the Lake District, scratched his head and said:

> *I've never seen anything like this anywhere else. I've spent 25 years of my working life entirely in property throughout the North West in a general practice, chartered surveyor role, and although I've seen umpteen different sorts of concrete prefabricated buildings, the majority dating from just after the Second World War when the building material shortage was on, I've never seen any built of cast iron before.*

Around him, deployed to astonishingly picturesque effects for such simple buildings, were the all-metal bungalows which won a tender from Manchester Corporation in 1929 when nineteen firms tendered for workmen's huts to house an army of labourers who were to build a controversial dam at Haweswater in the wild, mountainous countryside south-west of Penrith. All but one were for wooden cantonments which the city councillors feared would not stand up to the Lake District's notorious weather for the decade it would take to build a vast dam nearby. Roughly in the middle of the price range from £800 to £1,200 came the cast-iron kit buildings offered by Newton Chambers of Sheffield. Each weighed as much as two African elephants.

They were duly erected at the foot of Haweswater, only a couple of miles from the ancient village of Mardale Green which was due to vanish beneath the waters of the dam that the residents of the 'iron village', or Burnbanks as it was christened by Manchester Corporation, were to build over the next ten years. Supervised by a stern-looking police constable with an Alsatian called Tarzan, the sixty-six households, plus a couple of bunk dormitories initially for single men, welded a community along classic English village lines. They had sixpenny hops in the iron village hall on Friday nights, or sometimes Boris Karloff horror films or Felix the Cat, there were classes on Shakespeare from the Workers' Educational Association, a bowling green and allotments supplemented by forays up the valley for wild raspberries, mushrooms and nuts. The dam was delayed by recession but finally opened with due municipal ceremony in 1940, but the iron houses stayed on until very recent times, when two of them served as a base for the Royal Society for the Protection of Birds when England's only pair of golden eagles moved into the area in 1969. One of the birds is still there but most of the village is no more, apart from a neat cluster of replicas in modern materials built by Mr Paxman's company, and a fascinating account by the local historical society, *A Cast-Iron Community*. And so the sense of hamlet life goes on. As for the iron panels, there are examples preserved locally and in

Manchester for posterity, but the bulk of them may play a part in your life one day, in a different form. Paxman says: 'The rest went off in wagons to Liverpool docks and then disappeared off to China – the place that most scrap is heading for these days as we can't keep up with production. That's the way of the world.'

CHAPTER TEN

VILLAGE HAMPDENS
FACE THE FUTURE

In the 1960s when IT was born, everybody was supposedly going to
their cottage in the countryside to work in a virtual way.
LORD (RICHARD) ROGERS OF RIVERSIDE (1933–)

Where next then? The English village has entered the twenty-
first century in a comfier, smarter and more prosperous state
than ever before. It has problems and challenges, as has been the
case throughout the centuries, but now they are those of success.
Apart from coastal erosion, which nibbles away bungalows and
farms along parts of the North Sea coast at an almost visible rate,
it is hard to imagine the desertion of a rural community again.
The last brief and controversial examples were the hamlets West
End in North Yorkshire and Capel Celyn in North Wales which
followed the example of Mardale Green and Haweswater by
disappearing under the water of new reservoirs in the Washburn
and Afon Tryweryn valley in 1965/6. Public sentiment against
any damage to the countryside or familiar buildings is now
so strong that even the charms of a Little Chef restaurant at
Markham Moor which is one of the very few examples of a
1950s concrete hyperbolic paraboloid – a sweeping curve like a
Spanish Armada sailor's helmet – resulted in the diversion of a
new interchange on the A1 in Nottinghamshire.

This protection is reinforced by parish pump democracy which is the healthiest and most vigorous of all the layers of representation in England, from village meetings to the election of members of the European Parliament. The Coalition Government has drawn up a long slate of measures for its Localism Bill, whose title sums up the essence of village life, in theory if not necessarily in fact. One section which has attracted attention involves a range of referenda, designed to give local people more say on matters which for the last century and more have been the bread and butter of more distant councils at district and county level. The thinking behind it harks back to more distant times when 'pint pot parliaments' in village pubs took effective but very local decisions, in the context of more distant authorities – in the county town, cathedral close or even in far-away London – which had many more urgent tasks on their hands. It also draws on something of the idealism of the utopian communities set up in the countryside in times past, the Chartists, theosophists and Rowntree chocolate workers at their Moot Hall in York, who believed that a 'sense of village opinion' would emerge if sufficient people met together and went on discussing for long enough.

It remains to be seen whether this is well grounded or wishful thinking; meanwhile there are plenty of sceptics who worry that some of the measures which relax planning law will actually make life easier for housing developers. These are the agents of change most feared in the countryside, and their activities have been the target, overwhelmingly, of a curious power which was given to villages in the last great reform of local government in 1972. The Conservative Government of Edward Heath brought in the right of any civil parish in England to hold a referendum on anything, provided a minimum of six people call a meeting and the idea is then approved at the discussion by at least four others. The results are not binding on anyone but this tiny trigger can nonetheless lead to major consequences; the most recent one, in April 2011, saw so many villagers turn out to oppose a housing plan in Menston, in the green belt on the edge of Bradford and Leeds, that there were hour-long queues at the polling station. The local newspaper published pictures reminiscent of South Africa's first free election after independence and the pressure of the 98 per cent 'No' vote on Bradford City Council was considerable.

Interestingly, however, the power has been very little used, just a trickle of polls during the forty years and almost all of them to do with similar attempts to encroach on unspoiled land. The best-known was at East Coker in Somerset, the village made famous by giving its name to one of the poet T. S. Eliot's *Four Quartets*. In 2003 a referendum there was instrumental in preventing the building of 335 new houses, a proposal very similar to that at Menston, which at the time of writing remains undecided. Campaigners at Friends of the Earth believed that a 'forgotten' weapon had been unearthed and hailed the poll as 'the first of many more'. Instead, the countryside reverted to older methods of petitions, involvement of the local media and making such controversies the key issue at parish, district and county elections. Groups which monitor such things, including Friends of the Earth, now suggest that referenda are actually alien to the English, and particularly village, tradition of careful discussion; the very tradition invoked by the Government over its Localism Bill.

This is prime material for a pint-pot parliament to debate, but it sits well with the famous notion of stolid, persistent and cautious village democracy invoked by Thomas Gray in his *Elegy in a Country Churchyard*. Thinking of parochial church councils, elected churchwardens and the yeoman spirit of bowing the knee to no one, he wrote of

> *Some village Hampden that with dauntless breast*
> *The little tyrant of his fields withstood*
> *Some mute, inglorious Milton here may rest*
> *Some Cromwell guiltless of his country's blood.*

Hampden House, Great Hampden, Buckinghamshire

The original John Hampden, one of the leading Parliamentary opponents of King Charles I, was no fiery radical but a moderate and prudent statesman, albeit with a core of unshakeable principles which led him to take up arms in the end. He was also very much a product of the 'big house', whose influential role in local life has been so much part of the English village story. His birthplace of Hampden House still dominates the village of Great Hampden in Buckinghamshire, much aggrandized since his day but still with its fourteenth-century tower built of clunch, a distinctive local material formed by mixing mud and chalk stone. He died of wounds received at the battle of Chalgrove Field in 1643 but his family remained very much part of the establishment, and his son Richard was Chancellor of the Exchequer under William and Mary.

The fact that such an established member of the gentry, whose family claimed that their lordship of the manor dated to pre-Conquest times, is an icon of British democracy and the liberties of the subject has a bearing on the continuing success of the big house. Far from disappearing as Osbert Lancaster feared in his introduction to Ralph Dutton's *The English Country House* in 1935, the manors and mansions are flourishing, like the village itself, as never before. Even the largest of them all, Wentworth Woodhouse near Rotherham has returned to private hands after years as a PE teachers' training college. A London architect has embarked on the unnerving task of living in, and restoring, hundreds of rooms whose geography is so complex that house guests of the Earls of Fitzwilliam were given bags of confetti to lay a trail from the bedrooms to dinner, to find their way back like so many Hansels and Gretels.

More than this, the restrictions on building in the countryside which have grown ever tighter since the introduction of modern planning law in the 1947 Town and Country Planning Act, were relaxed very slightly but significantly in 1997. The Conservative Environment Secretary John Gummer issued a planning policy guidance (PPG) note allowing the building of houses of 'exceptional architectural merit' in rural settings. It was an invitation to the wealthy to revive the tradition of the grand country house.

Fewer than twenty have been built so far and all have faced difficult hurdles to jump with planning authorities. But the measure survived an attempt at repeal by Tony Blair's Labour Government in 2004, partly because of a successful exhibition of plans for seventeen new houses mounted by the Royal Institute of British Architects the previous year. Under the title of *The New English Country House*, it placed the proposed mansions in the context of some 1,500 'big houses' lost during the twentieth century, when economic and social conditions forced even the most tenacious and proud of their owners to give up the struggle with damp and leaking roofs. Designs included striking combinations of thatch and wraparound glass walls, as well as the more conventional pastiche of familiar long wings flanking a pediment resting on imposing columns. The scale of opportunity, and the resources required, was shown by Hungerford Park, an estate on the market for £13 million, with 2,000 acres, twenty-five cottages – and planning permission for an 18,000-square-foot neoclassical replacement for the Georgian and Victorian mansion demolished in the 1960s. Projects actually completed included the first PPG7 house, Wootton Hall at Ellastone in Staffordshire, a neoclassical commission by the Hon. Johnny Greenall of the Midlands brewing dynasty.

The exhibition's curator, the architectural historian Neil Guy, noted in the catalogue:

> What unites all the schemes without exception is the greatest care and attention taken with the landscape designs. They are all highly imaginative, yet context sensitive, and demonstrate such a depth of experience and richness of talent within the English landscape architecture discipline. Each scheme appears right for the house and right within its wider landscape context. This seemingly effortless harnessing of house and landscape remains an English tradition that continues to surprise and delight.

The architectural profession had an obvious interest, but many outside it agreed with the restoration and 'new classical' specialist Quinlan Terry when he told the *Daily Telegraph*:

> I can't see a problem. Country house-building suffered for 30 years after the war because people had a guilt complex about doing well: it was OK to spend your money on a yacht, but antisocial to build a decent house. There has always been the politics of envy. If you build something bad or grossly opulent, then you invite criticism, but something built well and with moderation has to be a good thing. The clause doesn't seem to have opened the floodgates for bad building and appears to be working perfectly well.

The main doubt now, nearly fifteen years after PPG7 was issued, is whether truly striking new large houses will emerge. When Hungerford Park came on the market, the estate agents Savills made encouraging noises about boldness, arguing not only that famous old mansions had often been built by successful City financiers, as was beginning to happen in the early twenty-first-century boom, but that 'no doubt Georgian houses would have been seen as radical and controversial in their day'. There was, however, the large and discouraging example of Eaton Hall in Cheshire, the country home of the Duke of Westminster. Although one of the country's richest people, the fifth Duke tired in the 1950s of maintaining the vast Gothic barracks built by Alfred Waterhouse, the architect of the Museum of Natural History in Kensington, and demolished most of it in 1963. Its chunky successor in Travertine marble by the architect (and brother-in-law to the duchess) John Dennys was truly radical. So much so, that in 1989 the sixth and current Duke encased it in a new facade reminiscent of a French chateau which was reckoned more sympathetic to the soft surrounding Cheshire landscape.

Another monster country home has added to doubts, the bizarre 'Hamilton Palace' in 100 acres of park near Uckfield which has taken an estimated £40 million at least of the money made by the controversial businessman Nicholas van Hoogstraten. Resembling a vast shopping mall with its golden dome and unlimited classical pastiche, the building appears to be in a constant state of construction and/or repair while its owner fights battles over footpath rights with the Ramblers' Association and building inspector reports which suggest that it will not be finished until 2020, if then. Van Hoogstraten has served jail sentences for organizing intimidation of business rivals and was convicted in 2002 of the manslaughter of one of them. Released after a successful appeal, he was ordered to pay the man's family £6 million compensation in a later civil case. In time, all this will no doubt become part of the extraordinary history of England's 'stately' homes.

The next biggest house in most villages, the rectory or vicarage, has entered the modern age in a very different state from its long transition in the past between successive clergy. The word 'Old' is increasingly often to be found in front of its name as the Church of England sells off large and valuable properties and rehouses incumbents in more modest homes. The market is so buoyant that a company such as Elite Prestige Property Search can boast: 'We only deal in £2 million-plus rectories' and splendid examples such as the Old Rectory at Burghfield in Berkshire, with its 16 acres and picturesque muddle of seventeenth-century and Victorian architecture, can be offered without the bat of an eyelid for £4,500,000. The eight bedrooms, five bathrooms and 10 acres of Newick rectory in East Sussex went for the same price in 2009, £2,000,000 up on its last previous sale ten years earlier.

Theologically, there seems little difficulty in Christian ministers giving up such earthly riches, and there are signs of other interesting social changes in villages as a result. These go beyond the creation of an 'extra manor house', sometimes exceeding the local hall in grandeur, to the character of the incumbents now coming into the countryside from theological colleges and curacies. The most astonishing change to an Anglo-Saxon or any villager for almost all the ensuing 1,500 years, would be that many are now women. That may well create changes, but it is more the complete absence of third sons of the gentry, the very few compilers of herbals or insect encyclopaedias, and the new clergy's energetic focus on church and community building which are setting markers for the villages' future. The only brake, apart from rural caution and English moderation, is that there are so many fewer incumbents. One 'new vicar' per parish might create a spiritual revolution – or a determined rebellion as happened when livings were confiscated and given to Puritan and radical divines during the seventeenth-century Cromwellian Interregnum. But today a rural ministry almost always serves a collection of parishes, sometimes with as many as a dozen different churches. The enormous imbalance of the historic church estate towards the countryside, with its thousands of historic and architecturally precious churches, also gives vicars and their parochial councils plenty to do.

The parish of Great Whitbourne in Herefordshire is a striking example, associated for centuries with the summer palace of the bishops of Hereford at Whitbourne Court. Those opulent days have long gone but the villages and hamlet of Edvin Loach, Tedstone Delamere, Upper Sapey, Wolferlow and Great Whitbourne itself have six historically important churches to care for. The best, at Upper Sapey, has had extensive repairs to reunite its roof with the partially Norman walls, but Wolferlow's lovely little building with its thirteenth-century carving of a veiled angel had no hope of raising tens of thousands of pounds and has closed. 'Don't be tempted to go inside to look at the angel or you might be in danger of joining her in heaven,' says its website. Edvin Loach has a Victorian church in good condition but also a roofless Saxon one which is only used once a year for a special service.

St James's Church, Tedston Delamere, Herefordshire

This catalogue sounds depressing but the congregation and clergy are full of energy. St James's church at Tedston Delamere, which has Norman tufa construction and interesting modern stained glass from the workshops of Hardman and Kempe, has been safeguarded by a particularly keen churchwarden, and the biggest of the parish's churches, St John the Baptist at Great Whitbourne, has seen a £218,000 fund-raiser which not only secured the dodgy masonry of the tower, but installed lavatories, a kitchen, an audio loop and extra space for village activities by moving the rood screen to the back of the church. More money is now being sought to restore a famous peal of bells dating back to 1717, both locally and from an impressive network of charities such as Rural Churches in Community Service and Music in Country Churches which often sees countryside concerts attended by its patron, that promoter of all things rural, the Prince of Wales.

Whitbourne's liveliness also saw the opening of a village community shop in 2007, financed in part by a local share issue with advice from the Plunkett Foundation, an immensely knowledgeable rural charity whose specialists include a team dedicated to sustaining existing shops in the countryside and finding ways of launching new ones. It sells apple juice from local farmer Ted Knight's orchard, honey from another villager's bees and steak, mince and burgers from Julia Evans's herd of Shorthorn cattle. The Live and Let Live, one of Whitbourne's two pubs, is next door.

Live and let live is itself an ideal which many English country pubs would dearly love to follow, in the face of a long period of attrition which in 2009 saw 893 pubs close across the UK, a rate of more than two a day of which about half were in the countryside. Many contributory causes have been blamed, from the dependence on car-driving customers who have to keep a careful eye on alcohol limits, to the national ban on smoking in pubs in 2007. More fundamental has been a decline in beer consumption to its lowest level since the 1930s, in the face of wine and other rival drinks, the availability of cheap drink at supermarkets and – less publicized than the others – a readjustment in the market after the 2005 Licensing Act. This allowed longer hours and other freedoms to landlords and stimulated competition for trade with the usual effect: well-run and imaginative country pubs have in general thrived while others have lost trade and gone to the wall. Finally, breweries and other owners of pub freeholds were tempted towards closure and sale for housing at the height of the property boom, but the banking crisis has made such windfall-seeking less common.

Thriving pubs almost invariably offer new services which benefit their village at a time when smaller populations and the huge growth in commuting to towns for work have seen other facilities disappear. Facing statistics such as the closure of English village schools at the rate of one a month between 1997 and 2008, or Royal Mail's programme of shutting 2,500 post offices across the country since 2008, landlords have stepped into the breach. And not just landlords. As with Winterbourne's community shop, villagers in Hudswell near Richmond in North Yorkshire – a paradise in terms of views where the Coast-to-Coast walk winds along Swaledale – have created a community cooperative and reopened the historic George and Dragon which closed in 2008 and was shuttered-up for a year. Inside the revived pub, Jackie and Margaret Stubbs offer a whirl of events and also The Little Shop, the first in Hudswell for thirty years.

Anne Waddington, who runs five thriving pubs in the Ilkley and Skipton area of North Yorkshire, has meanwhile introduced literary lunches, book circles, writing workshops, guided nature trails and a host of upmarket versions of that other great standby of the modern pub, the regular quiz. For all the gloom about closures, the enormous popularity of quizzes with questions craftily chosen from a bizarre range of subjects – the Old Testament followed by Goalkeepers of the 1950s – so that teams are essential, is itself a revival of the communal village spirit. Waddington has been helped by another success story: the revival of micro-brewing that has been overlooked in the annual budget moaning of Britain's brewers. Her pubs sell the range offered by a typical example, Ilkley Brewery, where production has risen 500 per cent since local beer enthusiasts Chris Ives and Stewart Ross gave up their previous jobs in surveying and planning to revive the old Ilkley Aerated Water Company two years ago. Hefty tax concessions for breweries making under 50,000 litres a year have seen them share in a national revival, much of it based in the countryside. In 1970, the UK had 140 micro-breweries, rising to 480 by 2004 and 767 by 2010.

This revival is reflected in the growing range of new industries in the countryside, where the decline of traditional village services such as shops and the 'Happy Families' collection of butcher, baker and so forth, has been balanced by telecottaging, small-scale manufacturing and in some cases very large firms. We have seen the effect of Gargrave's large bandage factory at Gargrave in the Yorkshire Dales; an even more spectacular example thrives on the edge of the county's other national parks, the North York Moors. Starting in 1934, a very well-hidden factory at Kirbymoorside built up a national reputation for designing and building small aircraft, eventually winning half of Britain's glider market and providing powered Firefly trainers for the US Air Force. Competition and recession caused a change of direction in the early twenty-first century, but this was equally spectacular. The firm now makes submersibles, including those which finally stopped the Gulf of Mexico oil spill. Since it is beautifully situated with ravishing properties available, good schools and excellent transport links, it has no difficulty attracting expert staff from the crowded, stressful likes of London.

The potential for rural work is as long as the list of things which the world wants or needs, and the cusp of the debate about village economies – doomed shells for the retired and wealthy, or thriving bases for the imaginative and energetic – is the subject of many a pint-pot parliament, and will remain so. Nor is it new. The beautiful village of Langton Green near Tunbridge Wells has lost three of its four pubs, one of its grocers, one of its butchers, both its police houses and the doctor's surgery. But who would have guessed that one of its residents, Peter Adolph, would invent a game called Subbuteo in 1946 and that painting the little table-sports figures would become a cottage industry? Such things come and go, as has been the nature of village life for 1,500 years, but it is unwise to be too apocalyptic, or too Pollyannish. Langton Green set up its own local society to protect rural amenities back in 1959.

The old staple of farming meanwhile remains fundamentally important to the national economy and the look of the English countryside, but much less so to the village economy. With so many fewer people employed, the old dependence of the community on the land has been broken. The relatively leisurely pace of agriculture between the world wars was also changed for ever by the exigencies of what amounted to a national siege between 1939 and 1944 and the dramatic increase in productivity led by state intervention. A successful campaign led to two million new acres going under plough to grow cereal crops by April 1940, with tractors working after dark using shielded blackout lamps and given special permission by Air Raid Precautions to plough on moonlit nights. By 1943 War Agricultural Committees known as WarAgs were directly farming 400,000 acres themselves. Organized initially at county level, WarAgs devolved as much as possible, setting up 500 district subcommittees with four to seven members who all lived locally. No committee had more than fifty farms to monitor and supervision was intense, as was enforcement of Government instructions. When a Hampshire farmer called Walden refused to plough up four acres of meadow to grow crops, he was shot by troops after a prolonged siege.

The sources of intervention have changed in the sixty-five years since the end of the Second World War, especially towards Europe, but not the essence of a tightly regulated and productive industry. As further mechanization and larger farms have reduced workforces, so they have also freed up buildings, from labourers' cottages to barns and outbuildings. These now form the basis of much diversification, ranging from maize-maze tourist attractions to ice cream manufacture and of course B&Bs – updated versions of the farm holidays which Beatrix Potter encouraged her tenants to take up around the village of Coniston in the Lake District when farming was insufficient to cope with the 1930s' Great Depression.

In many parts of the countryside, these activities often form farming's main encounters with the modern village: selling meat or vegetables to pubs and increasingly school kitchens which prize locally sourced fare, or working in tandem on tourist attractions. Tempting visitors to spend money in the countryside becomes ever-more ingenious. In Wiltshire, the peculiar annual phenomenon of neatly traced patterns of crushed crops in cornfields has led to brainwaves increasing income: Shredded Wheat hired a field to make an advertisement based on crop circles and pubs such as the Bridge Inn at Honeystreet sell locally brewed ales with names such as Alien Abduction and Away with the Fairies.

Amid these changes, village housing is flourishing as never before with prices which would strike dumb former residents of Honeysuckle, Sunnyside or even Moon Cottage – the last overlooking a former pub called The Moon in the village of Glaisdale on the North York Moors. This is good for the general appearance and overall prosperity of the countryside but brings with it the serious and much-discussed problem of excluding lower income residents, often including children brought up locally who compete in vain at the estate agents with, for example, wealthy buyers of second homes. Attempts to counter the usually inexorable workings of the market do not have an encouraging record, but there are several schemes in their infancy, including restrictive sale covenants imposed in several national parks on any newbuild.

The Yorkshire Dales National Park Authority has pioneered the approach, driven by average house prices of £240,000 compared with £102,000 in Bradford and £153,000 in Leeds. New housing must be sold only to local people – not always an easy definition – at below-market prices and may not be resold to others outside the category or as second homes or holiday lets. The jury is likely to be out for a while yet, and there are those who believe that the effect of second homes, which form some 15 per cent of properties in the Dales, is sometimes exaggerated, when many of them are sublet to other holidaymakers who bring both life and money to the area.

Much worse is high prices' encouragement of exclusive and sometimes even gated communities, based on a usually spurious fear of crime and disruption. Small fortresses more appropriate to the days of Stephen and Matilda or the Wars of the Roses have appeared in some parts of the countryside, particularly where a former hospital or school provides a set of convenient boundaries for automatic barriers and CCTV. Any scan of American 'villages' shows the ominous way in which this could develop; almost the polar opposite of the communal spirit and sense of fun which has lain for centuries at the heart of the feasts and frolics described earlier in this book.

These continue, overwhelmingly, in most parts of the country, with new 'traditions' joining ancient ones and frequent revivals of such ceremonies as Beating the Bounds taking on a modern twist. Community celebrations are well designed, too, for making wider points about village life and its twenty-first-century challenges. In the Cambridgeshire village of Shepreth in summer 2011, the annual fete featured the conversion of a redundant red telephone kiosk into a tiny pub called the Dog and Bone. Serving pints and three flavours of crisps in the cramped box, Alistair Janson explained that the stunt was part of a campaign over the local pub, The Plough, which had closed and was the subject of a hotly contested planning application for conversion into a house. In proper countryside style, the British Queen pub in the neighbouring village of Meldreth pitched in with drink, provisions and glasses.

Problems and prosperity, challenge and change; the English village faces up to all of them as the twenty-first century gets stuck into its second decade. It has great strength to fight its own battles, but also, thanks to the power of the 1,500 years of extraordinary history, a constituency all over the world which would never wish to see its spirit lost. This stretches as far as the Happy Global English Village in Taiwan, modelled on similar projects in Spain, Italy and South Korea which teach English to students in a supposedly authentic setting, complete with sessions on world music and dance, global awareness, cooking, and broadcasting. Perhaps these will indeed take their place, one day, in the ancient saga of maypoles and manor houses, cricket and crafts, thatch and mellow, sun-washed stone.

BIBLIOGRAPHY

There is an immense treasure store of literature on the English village, from the *Anglo-Saxon Chronicle* to twentieth-century masterpieces such as *Lark Rise to Candleford* by Flora Thompson and *Akenfield* by Ronald Blythe. This has been supplemented by TV, radio and the Internet to an equally copious extent. One of my own most lasting images of the downside of village life is a TV documentary in which a lugubrious rustic appeared at intervals describing another 'susanside', as he called the tragedy of neighbours who could not stand life any more. I have found the following sources extremely helpful and I am very grateful to their authors and publishers.

Ayerst, David, *The Guardian Omnibus 1821–1971* (Collins 1973)
Bampton & District History Society, *A Cast Iron Community* (2006)
Blair, Peter Hunter, *An Introduction to Anglo-Saxon England* (Cambridge University Press 1966)
Boston, Richard, *Beer and Skittles* (Collins 1976)
Boyd, Arnold, *The Country Diary of a Cheshire Man* (Collins 1946)
Bromyard & District Historical Society, *A Pocketful of Hops* (1988)
Bulmer, E. F., *Early Days of Cider Making* (Museum of Cider, Hereford 1980)
Calder, Angus, *The People's War: Britain, 1939–1945* (Jonathan Cape 1969)
Chadwick, Nora, *Celtic Britain* (Thames & Hudson 1963)
Challinor, Raymond, *The Struggle for Hearts and Minds* (Bewick Press 1995)
Cobbett, William, *Cobbett's England* (Parkgate 1997)
The Countryman magazine (various issues)
Cox, Charles J., *Parish Churches of England* (Batsford 1935)
Crookston, Peter, *The Pitmen's Requiem* (Northumbria Press 2010)
Daudy, Philippe, *Les Anglais – Portrait of a People* (Headline 1992)
Dutton, Ralph, *The English Country House* (Batsford 1935)
Epstein, James and Thompson, Dorothy, *The Chartist Experience* (1982)
Federation of Women's Institutes, *County Village Books* (various dates)
Forrest, A. J., *Masters of Flint Terence Dalton* (Lavenham 1983)

Gilbert, Sir Martin, *A Concise History of the Twentieth Century* (Harper Perennial 2002)

Greenoak, Francesca, *God's Acre: The Flowers and Animals of the Parish Churchyard* (Orbis 1985)

Hennell, T. *Change in the Farm* (Cambridge University Press 1934)

Jackson, Mary and Ken, *W. D. Campbell – Naturalist and Teacher* (The Wychwood Press 2003)

Jones, David, *Chartism and the Chartists* (Allen Lane 1975)

Kightly, Charles, *Country Voices: Life and Lore in Farm and Village* (Thames & Hudson 1984)

Kitteringham, Jennie, *Country Girls in 19th Century England* (History Workshop 1973)

Mead, Harry, *Inside the North York Moors* (David & Charles 1978)

Parker, Rowland, *The Common Stream* (Paladin 1976)

Pepper, Barrie, *A Haunt of Rare Souls* (Smith Settle 1990)

Rackham, Oliver, *The Illustrated History of the Countryside* (Weidenfeld & Nicholson 1994)

Royal Commission on the Historical Monuments of England, *Rural Houses of West Yorkshire 1400–1830* (HMSO 1986)

Scurr, Donald, *Root and Branch* (National Federation of Post Office and BT Pensioners 1999)

Skinner, John, *Journals of a Somerset Rector 1803–1834* (Oxford University Press 1984)

Tames, Richard, *England's Forgotten Past* (Thames & Hudson 2010)

Thomas, Keith, *Man and the Natural World* (Allen Lane 1983)

Thompson, Flora, *Lark Rise to Candleford* (Oxford University Press 1934)

Vale, Edmund, *Curiosities of Town and Countryside* (Batsford 1940)

Wainwright, Martin (ed.), *A Gleaming Landscape: A Hundred Years of the Guardian's Country Diary* (Guardian Books 2006)

Wainwright, Martin (ed.), *All Hands to the Harvest* (Guardian Books 2009)

Wainwright, Martin and Petrie, Ruth (eds) *The Guardian Book of the Countryside* (Guardian Books 2008)

Walford, Edward, *Village London* (Alderman Press 1983)

Warnett, Peter, *Three Mile Man* (Sweethaws 1980)

White, Gilbert, *The Illustrated Natural History of Selborne* (Thames & Hudson 1981)

Woodforde, John, *The Truth About Cottages* (Routledge & Kegan Paul 1969)

INDEX

(page numbers in italic type refer to illustrations)

INDEX

INDEX

INDEX